Criminal Justice
Recent Scholarship

Edited by
Marilyn McShane and Frank P. Williams III

A Series from LFB Scholarly

Disproportionate Confinement of African-American Juvenile Delinquents

John K. Mooradian

LFB Scholarly Publishing LLC
New York 2003

#5270650

Library of Congress Cataloging-in-Publication Data

Mooradian, John K., 1953-
  Disproportionate confinement of African-American juvenile
delinquents / John K. Mooradian.
    p. cm. -- (Criminal justice)
Includes bibliographical references and index.
ISBN 1-931202-69-9 (alk. paper)
  1. Discrimination in juvenile justice administration--United States.
2. Juvenile detention--United States. 3. African American juvenile
delinquents. I. Title. II. Criminal justice (LFB Scholarly Publishing
LLC)
  HV9104.M66 2003
  364.36'089'96073--dc22

2003016256

ISBN 1-931202-69-9

Printed on acid-free 250-year-life paper.

Manufactured in the United States of America.

Table of Contents

1 OVERVIEW   1
  Purpose of the Study   2
  Organization of the Book   5

2 DISPROPORTIONATE CONFINEMENT OF AFRICAN-
  AMERICAN MALE DELINQUENTS   7
  Research on Disproportionate Minority Confinement   8
  Afrocentric Perspective   11
  Special Circumstances of African-American Youth   13

3 MAJOR DEVELOPMENTS IN DELINQUENCY
  INTERVENTION, POLICY, AND THEORY   17
  The Invention of Delinquency   19
  The Quest for Cause   20
  Imperatives for Intervention   22
  Changing the Child   23
  Creation of the Juvenile Court   26
  Modern Practice Approaches   26
  Modern Policy Approaches   36
  Emergent Theories of Delinquency   37

4 SOCIAL ECOLOGY AND JUVENILE DELINQUENCY   41
  The Relationship of Stress and Coping to Delinquency   42
  The Relationship of Family Functioning to Delinquency   49

5   PROBLEM, PARTICIPANTS, AND PROCEDURES   57
    Statement of the Problem   57
    Participant Sample   59
    Data Management Procedures   59
    Research Design   61
    Measures   62
    Variables and Operational Definitions   79
    Planned Analyses   82

6   RELATIONSHIPS AMONG VARIABLES   85
    Research Questions   85
    Psychometrics of Clinical Assessment Instruments   88
    Description of Sample   98
    Correlational Analysis   111
    Multiple Regression Analysis   123

7   INTERPRETATIONS AND IMPLICATIONS   137
    Measurement Issues   137
    Intake Characteristics of the Sample   139
    Delinquent Behavior and Out-of-Home Placement   141
    Expected Associations with Out-of-Home Placement   142
    Additional Associations with Out-of-Home Placement 143
    Other Notable Associations   146
    Explanation of Multiple Placements   146
    Explanation of Duration of Placement   147
    Delimitations and Limitations of the Study   147
    Implications for Systems Dynamics   149
    Implications for Juvenile Justice Policy   154
    Implications for Juvenile Justice Practice Intervention 156
    Conclusion   156

NOTES   159

APPENDICES   171

REFERENCES   179

INDEX   201

Acknowledgements

I am indebted to Brother James Caley, csc, who encouraged me to pursue the skills necessary to write this book. Steve Kapp helped me understand the value of applied research, and nurtured a great friendship in the process. David Lounsbury provided knowledge, skill, and encouragement that sustained me through this analysis.

Rena Harold and Gary Anderson supported me fully in this opportunity to share my work.

This book is dedicated to the families who raise children in our most challenging environments.

CHAPTER 1
Overview

Placement of children and adolescents out of their family homes has a long history in the United States. Indeed, removing young people from their homes has been the "treatment of choice" for almost two hundred years. Out-of-home placement has been favored, especially, for those minors who violate the law.

Although such a practice may provide particular advantages in provision of control, it also produces accompanying limitations on personal freedoms, which should be considered carefully in a free society. When young people are removed from their families and placed in institutions, detention facilities, residential care, or community-based group homes, they face sweeping changes in their living situation. In the United States, most of these settings are established to provide rehabilitation services, and many offer a combination of educational, vocational, and psychological services. While the quality of these services varies, as does their effectiveness, the reality is that removal from home constitutes a serious life change for many youth. In this way, it becomes clear that out-of-home placement represents a major influence in the lives of the young people so treated.

This book emerges from a belief that the differential impact of this practice for vulnerable groups should be understood from an informed perspective. In addition, the practice of placing young people who offend in non-family settings raises questions of justice for both these offenders and their victims. For the offenders, there are matters of maintenance of due process protections in juvenile justice decision-making, optimization of length of stay in placement, safeguarding against construction of delinquent careers through prolonged exposure to other offenders, provision of adequate resources for rehabilitation, and control of negative impacts on family relationships.

For victims of juvenile crime and for society at-large, there is a need to control antisocial behavior, establish a sense of restitution for injury or loss, and deter future crimes. The right of citizens to live free from criminal intrusion is a cornerstone of our social principles.

When one considers that many of the youth who are placed out of the home are poor, of racial or ethnic minority status, or otherwise potentially disenfranchised, matters of equity in decision-making and the application of social power emerge. American history demonstrates that members of the "underclass", especially in urban environments, are most likely to be removed from their families. This practice is not only historical. It prevails today.

PURPOSE OF THE STUDY
In the 1988 amendments to the Juvenile Justice and Delinquency Prevention Act of 1974, the federal government required that states participating in the Formula Grants Program move to reduce disproportionate confinement of African-Americans, American Indians, Asians, Pacific Islanders, and Hispanics, in any jurisdiction where it was found (Pope, Lovell, & Hsia, 2002). The predominant racial or ethnic minority group in juvenile justice settings is African-American males.

Focus on African-American Males
This study was undertaken to better understand the problem of disproportionate confinement of African-American adolescent males in juvenile justice settings. African-American males are more likely to be placed out of the home than their European-American counter-parts, and to be escalated to more restrictive placements for relatively less serious offenses (Snyder & Sickmund, 1999). Many African-American males, once placed out of their homes, also face a compounding process of continued confinement, as decision- makers employ escalating forms of social control (Snyder & Sickmund, 1999). The work documented in this book centers on out-of-home placement as a representation of confinement. This form of confinement involves

placement in a setting that is neither the youth's own family home (adoptive, blood-related or fictive), nor a "family-like" setting such as regular foster care. Further, this type of confinement means that the young man has been placed in a detention facility, a "residential care" facility, or a restrictive group home setting.

The number of out-of-home placements is counted for each youth, and this investigation examines variables associated with accumulation of out-of-home placements and the duration of the most recent placement, for a sample of African-American male delinquents. It was undertaken to improve understanding of the factors associated with the observed higher confinement rates for minority, especially African-American, youth.

The author's motivations for completing this study represent a range of personal and professional concerns. Experience in the field with delinquents and their families fuels not only a professional curiosity about the relationship of the included variables, but also a personal commitment to improving the operation of a system that attempts to meet the dual needs of social control and social treatment. In both treatment-oriented and correctional settings, it has proven difficult to integrate public safety and effective interpersonal intervention.

Work with involuntary clients in highly restrictive environments highlights issues of self-determination and social control. Due to socially intolerable behavior, authority structures make decisions that limit the freedom of individuals for the good of society, by requiring them to live in specified and controlled settings. For many of the young people who are placed into such facilities, this is the most disruptive experience of their young lives. It has been observed to have profound implications for family relationships, further offending, and emotional and cognitive development (Barton & Butts, 1990; Kapp & Schwartz, 1994). While social control may require such a removal from home in many cases, this practice should be well informed and balanced by knowledge of the paths and processes involved.

Cultural sensitivity sharpens a focus on the particular vulnerability of African-American male youth to policies favoring out-of-home placement and external control. Professional values, including the need for effective treatment, respect for the dignity and worth of the person and concern for human welfare, and, especially, a concern with social justice, underlie this attempt to deepen available knowledge and illuminate possible alternatives for intervention at the treatment and policy levels.

In the present work, a conscious decision was made to illuminate the factors that are specifically related to the situation of African-American males who experience multiple out-of-home placements. Ya Azibo (1992) warns researchers of the "practical problem of hegemony". He cites others as noting that a characteristic behavior of Europeans is to judgmentally compare different people to themselves, using themselves as a standard. The reader may reject this statement as overgeneralization, or worse, but it, nonetheless, presents a case for specialized research to illuminate the circumstances of African-Americans without relying entirely on race comparisons. Ya Azibo also presents "axioms of comparative research", which include an assertion that it is proper to make racial comparisons only when the racial groups are equated on all relevant variables, especially culture. Further, it is noted that whenever constructs are used, culture is a relevant variable. This study examines variables such as offense history and number of placements, but also employs culturally determined constructs such as stress, coping, and family functioning. These "axioms" support an approach that recognizes the distinct experiences of African-American and European-American youth.

This study applies a systemic framework and ecological orientation to find a fit of factors at the individual, family, community, and juvenile justice system levels, in order to explain forms of out-of-home placement for African-American male delinquents. Existing quantitative data at each level, from a large multi-site agency, were analyzed with techniques that are appropriate for ecological understanding. The psychometric properties of the clinical assessment instruments used by the agency were examined to determine their appropriateness for this sample. Primary analyses use descriptive, correlational, and regression techniques. Preliminary work for path analysis is presented, and disproportionate minority confinement is discussed from a systems dynamics perspective to realistically represent the feedback inherent in the social ecology of the participants.

Existing research provides a basis for this investigation as described below, but also evidences notable gaps in specific knowledge of the environmental and personal characteristics of African-American male delinquents. Although the analyses undertaken in this study are subject to limitations on generalization, and suffer from less than perfect psychometrics, they offer knowledge about this particular sample of participants and serve to explicate relevant ecological relationships.

Research Questions
The specific research questions investigated in this study include the following:

1. What personal, family, and environmental characteristics describe African-American male delinquents who experience out-of-home placements?

2. What are the observed associations of personal, family, and environmental variables for African-American male delinquents who experience out-of-home placements?

3. Which sets of variables best explain out-of-home placements for African-American male delinquents?

Within its limitations, this study is intended to have value for practice, policy, and further research. Findings should be applied tentatively, but they offer incremental information for directing clinical intervention and prevention with African-American youth that centers on reducing the undesirable impacts of personal, familial, and ecological factors. Policy decisions focused on reduction of disproportionate minority confinement may be supported by clearer specification of the factors that can be controlled to stem the tide of confinement.

Implications for further research include identification of potentially relevant variables that are not addressed in this study, suggestions for improved measurement, and explication of foci for qualitative study.

ORGANIZATION OF THE BOOK
This work is organized in a way that is intended to introduce the reader to several interrelated aspects of the social ecology of African-American delinquent males, describe the procedures used to conduct the study, and then present and discuss specific findings for further application.

Three brief chapters set the context for the study through review of the current state of knowledge about disproportionate minority confinement, development of practice and policy, and research on the ecological factors that are included in this study.   Chapter Two summarizes the current state of knowledge about disproportionate minority confinement, and the Afrocentric perspective.   The third chapter outlines the historical context of out-of-home placement of delinquent youth, including modern policy and practice developments, and emergent theories that purport to explain delinquent behavior.   The fourth chapter presents research on the relevant ecological variables such as stressors, coping strategies, and family functioning. Additional chapters present the structure and findings of the study. The fifth chapter offers a statement of the problem and describes the methodology and research techniques used to conduct this investigation.   Chapter Six details characteristics of the youth in the study sample, depicts a profile of the typical youth in this group, identifies significant relationships between included variables, presents a set of correlational schematics that show observed relationships between levels of the ecological system, and evaluates various regression models designed to explain forms of out-of-home placement. Chapter Seven critically discusses the study findings, and outlines implications for future investigations, policy, and practice.

CHAPTER 2

Disproportionate Confinement of African-American Male Delinquents

Differential disposition of juvenile cases involving European-American and African-American youth has been identified as a long-standing problem of significant proportion (Hsia & Hamparian, 1998). Charges of racial discrimination in juvenile court proceedings were initially raised during the Civil Rights movement of the late 1960's (Ferdinand, 1991). Subsequent policy measures were enacted, including the Juvenile Justice and Delinquency Prevention Act of 1974. This act, as amended in 1988 and 1992, issues a mandate to reduce over-representation of minority youth in confinement. The timelines for compliance have been extended, however, and results vary by state (Howell, 1998). Despite efforts on the federal and state levels, African-American delinquent youth continue to be overrepresented in secure settings when compared to their European-American counterparts.

The administrator of the Office of Juvenile Justice and Delinquency Prevention has stated that an effective juvenile justice system should treat every offender as an individual and provide needed services to all (Bilchik, 1998). A persistent inequity in disposition of cases associated with race masks individual difference, brings real human consequences, and counters such a system goal. Concern with the problem of over-representation of African-American youth in restrictive settings has led

7

to acceptance of the term "disproportionate minority confinement" (Hsia & Hamparian, 1998).

RESEARCH ON DISPROPORTIONATE MINORITY CONFINEMENT

By now, the reader may have encountered the often-cited statistic that one of every three black men in his twenties in America is either incarcerated, on parole, or on probation (Maurer & Huling, 1995). This information, alone, speaks to the seriousness of the overall problem of young African-American men being locked away from their families and communities. While this observation describes the situation for young adults, the existence of inordinate incarceration rates for African-American juveniles has also been empirically established.

The bulk of published research on the phenomenon of disproportionate minority confinement centers on establishing and amplifying the extent of the problem. Other related studies offer limited insight into causes, potential interventions, and broader policy implications.

McGarrell (1993), in a study of differential confinement rates across the states, found that those states with expanding "non-White" populations have tended to incarcerate juveniles at a higher rate since the mid-1970's compared to those states whose proportions have remained relatively steady. This finding is interpreted to mean that increased levels of punitive responses to juvenile crime are linked to heterogeneity in the population, which could indicate discriminatory practices.

Prevalence studies were conducted to outline the scope of the problem of disproportionate minority confinement. These studies estimated that one in seven African-American males would be confined prior to his 18th birthday, while the estimate for European-American youth was only one in 25 (Hsia & Hamparian, 1998). Another study indicates that African-American males of all ages are seven to ten times more likely to be incarcerated than comparable groups of European-Americans (Brinson, 1994). While these investigations were based on national data and yielded only estimations as results, they provide some support for the conclusion that minority youth continue to be disproportionately confined.

The Office of Juvenile Justice and Delinquency Prevention (Sickmund, Snyder, & Poe-Yamagata, 1995) concluded that African-American youth are significantly over-represented at all levels of the juvenile justice system. African-American youth comprise only 15% of the United States' population aged ten to seventeen, yet they represent 25% of all juvenile arrests, 49% of the known violent offenses committed by juveniles, 36% of the total adjudicated juvenile cases, 41% of youth in detention facilities, 46% of youth in long-term public institutions, and 52% of juvenile cases waived to adult criminal court. A review of these percentages also indicates that African-American youth are dealt with in a more restrictive fashion within the system, than are European-American youth, who make up a much higher percentage of the total juvenile arrests.

In addition, these data appear to show that African-American youth are at increasing risk for inclusion in the system. In 1983, minority youth represented 53% of the population in secure juvenile corrections facilities, and by 1996, the figure had increased to 68% (Sickmund, Snyder, & Poe-Yamagata, 1997). Between 1986 and 1995, the number of open delinquency cases involving European-American youth increased by 34%, while those of African-American youth increased by 72% (Sickmund, Snyder, & Poe-Yamagata, 1995).

The only known longitudinal study of delinquents released from residential care who were subsequently imprisoned in adult correctional facilities also provides relevant findings (Kapp, Schwartz, & Epstein, 1994). For this sample of youth released from a private residential program in Michigan, background and intake variables such as race, family demographics, age, county of commitment, legal status (delinquent, abused/neglected, status offender), number and types of previous placements, and type of prior offense history showed no significant correlation with subsequent imprisonment as an adult. Similar findings were evident for treatment related variables such as type of residential program (campus or community-based), amount and type of treatment contacts with the family, and number of times a youth truanted from the program. Even more striking is the lack of significant correlation between treatment outcome measures, such as completion of treatment goals and type of placement at discharge, and adult imprisonment.

Adopting a delinquency typology originally presented by Wolfgang, Figlio, and Sellin (1972), which structures identification of repeat offenders as 'recidivists', Kapp and his colleagues (1994) found that earlier conclusions regarding juvenile recidivists being more likely to commit future crimes also extend into adulthood, and provide some evidence for the concept of an ongoing and dynamic criminal career. In addition to bivariate analyses, their study used logistic regression and event history analysis to examine the predictive value of a combined delinquency/race typology and found that being a "non-White" juvenile recidivist placed outside the family home post-release, was significantly related to higher likelihood of adult imprisonment. These youth had nearly a one in five chance of being imprisoned as adults, while White juvenile non-recidivists who return to their families were four and one-half times less likely to find their way into the adult prison system. Kapp, Schwartz and Epstein (1994) focused on the interaction of race, delinquent activity, family influences, and confinement. These results may also inform the eventual construction of a dynamic model by illuminating the effects of repeated adjudications and confinements. Moreover, the prior study convincingly demonstrates the dynamic nature of confinement of African-American youth even as it is extended into adulthood.

Pope and Feyerherm (1990) conducted a meta-analysis of literature published on disproportionate minority confinement between 1969 and 1989. They found 46 studies, all of which showed the presence of substantial differences in the processing of minority youth within a variety of juvenile justice settings. Approximately two thirds of the reviewed research indicated that a youth's racial status made a difference at selected stages of juvenile justice processing. These studies used a broad range of research methods. In addition, it was determined that differential outcomes by race could occur at any stage of juvenile processing, and that they grew more pronounced the further involved the youth became in the juvenile justice system.

Pope, Lovell, and Hsia (2002) replicated this meta-analysis for studies published between 1989 and 2001. They located 34 studies that focused on minority youth, 27 of which included African-Americans. Perhaps due to increased measurement specificity and narrower operational definitions since the 1970's and 1980's studies, the second meta-analysis found more "mixed results" by race in the form of interactions. About half of the reviewed studies reported direct race effects on juvenile processing, and several more included factors such as family and community characteristics, or local political system issues, which might overlap with racial factors, which were interpreted as indirect or mixed results.

Reported results of the included studies indicate that African-American youth receive harsher judgments at the petition phase, and more restrictive placements at the detention, petition, and disposition phases (Johnson & Secret, 1990; Leiber, 1994; Austin, Leonard, Pope, & Feyerherm, 1995; Bridges, Conley, Engen, & Price-Spratlen, 1995; Feld, 1995; Frazier & Bishop, 1995; Leiber & Jamieson, 1995; Wordes, Bynum, & Conley, 1995; Bridges & Steen, 1998). Wu, Cernovich, and Dunn (1997) found that although European-American youth in their study were more likely to be adjudicated, African-American youth were more likely to be detained or placed. Decomo (1998) found a higher rate of arrest and confinement for African-American youth as compared to European-American youth.

AFROCENTRIC PERSPECTIVE
The Afrocentric perspective has been applied to many social issues. It is based on a distinction between African and European worldviews, and can be traced to traditional African cultures that predated the influence of European colonization and imperialism (Scheile, 1997). These African cultures emphasized collective identity over individualism; emotional and spiritual connection over material objectification; equal distribution of resources over concentration of resources among those perceived to have contributed the most; and reciprocal interdependent responsibility of the government and the individual over dichotomous government and individual responsibility. Meyers (1992) characterizes the Afrocentric perspective as truly holistic, because it embraces both spiritual and material realities simultaneously. A view of the "extended self" is described as encompassing one's ancestors, the yet unborn, the community, and all of nature. Knowledge is viewed as "self knowledge" wherein a person's perceptions are considered to be accurate representations of the interconnected reality among all persons and all of nature.

The Afrocentric perspective also emphasizes an inclusion of racial and ethnic pride by highlighting the often-overlooked contributions of

African cultures. Afrocentrism has been presented as a source of strength and positive cultural identity for African-Americans.

From an Afrocentric point of view, Brinson (1994) considers several explanations for higher arrest and confinement rates among African-Americans. Listed are family structure, school performance, values, peer relationships, media influences, "racial features", and personality factors. Brinson reasons that socio-economic status, academic achievement, childhood patterns, and coping styles are interrelated and serve as the most important determinants of maladaptive behavior in African-American youth. Although he presents no empirical data of his own, he intersperses his arguments with relevant findings from other investigations that support his points. While such an approach may not meet stringent standards for scholarly research, his discussion dispenses valuable nuggets of knowledge, that warrant further examination. Included are the assertions that approximately two-thirds of African-American children live in poverty; the education level of mother and the length of father presence are the best predictors of academic achievement among Black children; that seven to nine year-old offenders are more likely to be non-White and living with a single mother than White or having two parental figures; and that those youth who accept the cultural goals of society but are excluded from the means to achieve them are more likely to turn to crime. The attribution of higher confinement rates to these factors raises other empirical questions, but also emphasizes the potential role of the social ecology of the offender in the development of individual behaviors, and juvenile justice system dispositions.

It has also been argued that African-American male adolescents comprise an "endangered species", in part, due to being mislabeled and ignored by the mental health system (Gibbs, 1989). From this perspective, the misbehavior of many of these youth, which could be interpreted as symptoms of psychiatric problems, lodges them in the juvenile justice system instead of the mental health system. Such a process would swell the ranks of African-American juvenile delinquents, and produce increased levels of confinement, by displacing these youth from the mental health arena.

Most efforts directed toward understanding delinquency among African-American youth have been based on samples that predominantly include European-American youth. One exception attempts to distinguish the pathways that lead toward delinquency by racial group (Loeber, Wung, Keenan, Giroux, Stouthammer-Loeber, Van Kammen, & Maughan, 1993). These researchers found that African-American youth were more likely to begin their path to delinquent careers with aggressive behavior such as fighting and gang fighting, while European-American youth were more likely to exhibit annoying and bullying behavior, before proceeding to fighting.

SPECIAL CIRCUMSTANCES OF AFRICAN-AMERICAN YOUTH

Other bodies of research indicate that African-American youth encounter factors in life that either are not contacted by European-American youth, or which do not hold the same level of personal impact. Two such factors are racism and exposure to interpersonal violence.

Racism

It may be argued that racism is at the root of any discrepancies in the rates of social problems that affect African-Americans and European-Americans. Further, as an ideology, racism operates at the meta-level of social systems and pervades the American social ecology (Goldberg & Hodes, 1992). Seen from this perspective, the topic of racism is far too broad to address within the scope of this book, but it is instructive to deal with the forms of impact it may exert on the immediate environment of the youth, such as the family functions of cohesion and control.

Goldberg and Hodes (1992) examined families of Black substance-abusing youth. With a recognition of the potential for oppression in modern society, they sought particular developmentally significant issues for minority families who are negotiating the transition of adolescent children to autonomy. Of note were two oppositional, and potentially problematic, patterns that have been elsewhere related to delinquency. Encounters with racism could strengthen the external boundary of the family, thereby propelling parents and adolescents toward each other, and increasing levels of enmeshment as family members unite against an external threat. The mechanism cited in dysfunctional examples of this process is parental "over-protectiveness", which embodies aspects of family cohesion and parental control. Alternatively, racism could drive the adolescent farther away from the parents in pursuit of a break from family patterns as a way of belonging to an accepting and powerful group, thereby increasing levels of family disengagement. In this circumstance, family cohesion drops below a functional level, and the balancing effects of parental control are overcome as the adolescent draws inordinate personal power. The authors conclude that racism can be considered in terms of the balance between the centripetal (inwardly propelling) and centrifugal (outwardly propelling) forces in family relationships that are central to individual development.

Interpersonal Violence
Encounters with violence are an inescapable part of the social landscape for many African-American youth in urban environments, especially males. Violence touches these young people as both victims and perpetrators. African-American youth are three to five times more likely than European-Americans to become murder victims; African-American teenagers commit about 80% of the violent crimes suffered by their peers; and 90% of the time, the offenders and victims are males (King, 1997).

Violence emerges as a prominent feature when one attends to the verbalizations of certain African-American delinquent youth. In a provocative qualitative account of the experience of gang members in the city of Detroit, Taylor (1990) provides several direct quotations that demonstrate the experience of both being subjected to violence and perpetrating violent acts on others. From an 18 year old, comes the following (Taylor, 1990, p. 56):

> I likes to bust heads. Violence? What's that? You got to dog everybody, or they gonna dog you. Doggin' is my specialty...I dogs men, boys, girls, bitches, my momma, teachers, policemen, policebitches, my momma's boyfriends. I'll just see somebody and start doggin' them in the street.

From an Afrocentric perspective, King (1997) identifies the history of chattel slavery, institutional racism, and poverty as factors contributing to this condition. He observed that one in three Africans died on the march to the coast, and another one-third died during the sea voyage in the enslavement period. Lynching survived abolition, as is well documented in accounts of such public displays of violence against African-American males. Police brutality and disproportionate use of capital punishment are included as examples of official violence.

Racial discrimination and poverty are perpetuated by limited involvement of African-American youth in the opportunity structures of American life. King (1997, p. 89) states, "African-American boys...know that if they cannot dribble a basketball, hit a baseball, or sack a quarterback, this country has little use for them...". He also indicts the popular 'warrior mentality', and the related war paradigm, as a pervasive metaphor in American life which undermines a culturally and socially appropriate value system. King concludes with a linkage of these ecological factors to the personal factors of low self-worth, lack of purpose, lack of social competencies for a hostile environment, lack of connectedness in the African-American community, and lack of a culturally specific and relevant world-view.

Violence among African-American youth has been described as a socio-cultural phenomenon by Cousins (1997). Through qualitative research, he locates violence within the contexts of life in a poor, black, urban high school and community. These contexts are heavily shaped by culture, which provides the shared meanings of events and interactions. He argues that public policy, as reflected in several specific pieces of legislation enacted since the late 1960's, deals with the violence of African-American youth as somehow separate from the violence that is woven into the fabric of American life. This separate treatment, he further argues, results in attributions of personal aberrance rather than reflection of poverty and racial discrimination in contact with mainstream culture.

Afrocentric observers emphasize the important role of culture in shaping shared beliefs, personal experiences, and the perceptions that direct social power. As is made apparent in the next chapter, these cultural forces have long been at work in the juvenile justice arena. A careful review of historical factors suggests that prevailing prejudices about certain groups of people, personal responses to restricted social resources, and the extension of social control into the lives of individuals and families may have changed form over the past two hundred years, but little has changed in their essential functions.

CHAPTER 3

Major Developments in Delinquency Intervention, Policy, and Theory

The evolution of confinement as the method of choice for dealing with juvenile crime provides a useful backdrop for an investigation of disproportionate minority confinement. The choice to incarcerate any children facilitates the choice to incarcerate selected groups of children at inequitable rates. The problem of disproportionate minority confinement, thus, may be understood as a current manifestation of long-standing social forces.

In relation to juvenile crime, a caring society addresses, what are often perceived to be, the opposing needs for social control and social treatment. Based on such a perception, the value of safety for society is juxtaposed with the value of humane treatment and socialization of the youthful offender. Rather than viewing these needs as adversarial forces in a dialectical process, however, it may be more useful to recognize their symmetrical operation, and to organize them in the structure of a double helix as depicted in Figure 1.

Such a diagram represents an attempt to illustrate the connection between these needs in a way that realistically matches the experience of history. Although proponents of social control are often at odds with those who favor social treatment, the forces themselves appear to be systemically-linked. Historical evidence, as presented in the remainder

17

**Figure 1: Symmetrical Structure of Social Control and Social
Treatment**

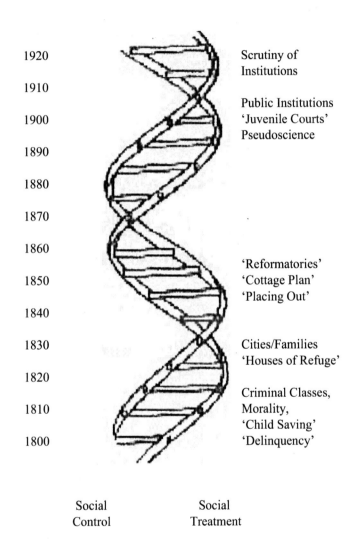

1920	Scrutiny of Institutions
1910	
	Public Institutions
1900	'Juvenile Courts'
	Pseudoscience
1890	
1880	
1870	
1860	
	'Reformatories'
1850	'Cottage Plan'
	'Placing Out'
1840	
1830	Cities/Families
	'Houses of Refuge'
1820	
	Criminal Classes,
1810	Morality,
	'Child Saving'
1800	'Delinquency'

Social   Social
Control   Treatment

of this chapter, reflects ongoing attempts to balance these social obligations, and may be interpreted to show that each significant development of the juvenile justice system has incorporated them in a pattern of linkage rather than conflict. This evidence is considered below.

THE "INVENTION" OF DELINQUENCY

Although concern for children and the experience of juvenile crime did not begin out of the darkness in the early nineteenth century, prior to that time there was no systematic separation of juveniles from other criminals in the United States (Montgomery, 1909; Bruno, 1957). "Delinquency" was a term that was applied to all those in the "dangerous classes" who committed crimes, regardless of their age.

It has been suggested that specialized application of the term to juvenile offenders began to extend governmental control over a range of youthful activity that had previously been ignored or dealt with informally (Platt, 1977). With the rise of industrialization, families were drawn to urban centers to secure employment. In conjunction with this concentration of population, and parents working away from the home, came the advent of public education.

These developments created opportunities for children to become a greater social nuisance as they came together in consolidated peer groups (Ferdinand, 1991). If children committed crimes, they were initially dealt with by the criminal justice system and sometimes incarcerated along with adults, but such a practice did not allow effective intervention with the numbers of troublesome youth whose behavior fell short of felonious activity. Ferdinand (1991) argues that a means of bolstering the authority of the family and the school, in this context, was the construction of a new social status known as the "juvenile". He notes that the family and school retained a primary responsibility to socialize children, and the doctrine of *parens patriae* was used to legitimate the intercession of the state in cases where the primary means of control had failed.

A concern with the impact of juvenile crime caught the attention of a group of people who have come to be known as the "child-savers" (Pumphrey & Pumphrey,1961). Much of the work of the child-savers was delineated by the view of the child as a helpless victim of the excesses and inequities of society, but a dangerous victim nonetheless

(Bruno, 1957). If unchecked, this victim could wreak havoc with pleasant society. Within these positions, it is possible to identify the earliest expressions of the need for social control and humane treatment methods that were intended to change individual behaviors. The seeds of connection between a punitive external control perspective and a more benign treatment orientation were sown at this early juncture and persist to the present day.

THE QUEST FOR CAUSE

Much effort during the nineteenth century was directed toward identifying and outlining the causes of social problems, in order to apply increasing social resources to their redress. Crime was a troubling social problem, and criminality became a focus for such investigation. Activity of this nature was focused on construction of an explanation for the emergence of the "criminal classes" (Pumphrey & Pumphrey, 1961).

Among the earliest identified causes of delinquency were the personal attributes of individual delinquents. Disadvantaged children living in cities were regarded as "intellectual dwarfs" and "physical and moral wrecks" (Platt, 1977). A theory of personal predisposition to crime was popularized.

The Chaplain of the New York House of Refuge (Pierce, 1869, p. 25) wrote:

> ...young criminals, now numbered by the thousands...have fallen into crime, not through the want, as we have seen, of excellent homes, but through peculiar weakness or corrupting influences. Poor blood, low moral culture, the pinch of poverty, the habit of indulgence, pre-dispose this class to early crime.

Although such an explanation smacks of stereotyping and "blaming the victim" from a more modern perspective, it maintained favor at the time of its proposition.

Later, the urban poor family was also indicted as a cause of delinquency. In the first circular of the Children's Aid Society published in 1853, Charles Loring Brace noted that the Society was to become a means of dealing with the "...increasing crime and poverty of the destitute classes of New York". He continued to say that the poor and immigrant children "...were unable to share in what we should call a home." (Pumphrey & Pumphrey, 1961, p. 123). Such remarks illustrate a view that breakdown of the family was a primary factor in the production of juvenile delinquents. Also inherent in such a perspective, is the belief that immigrant and poor families somehow abdicated their responsibility to provide moral training and behavioral control for their children. These attitudes toward the recognized underclass echo in more recent characterizations of low income, urban, African-American families who replaced immigrants in the social strata one hundred years later.

Conditions in industrialized cities were eventually identified as a set of explanations for juvenile crime as well. Cities were generally regarded as crowded and unpleasant places for all but the very rich. Segregation by ethnic group, religion, and social class were escalating throughout the mid-nineteenth century (Leiby, 1978). The city was seen by many as the breeding ground of criminal activity. Julia Lathrop wrote that "....we take the sturdiest of European peasantry and at once destroy in a large measure its power to rear to decent livelihood that first generation of offspring upon our soil" (Platt, 1977, p. 92).

By the late nineteenth century, concerns about the urban environment and the culpability of families and individuals were drawn together in a cohesive explanation. The prevailing epistemology was one of "science", wherein everything was explained, no longer through religious imagery, but through secular, empirical, and rational constructions (Platt, 1977; Leiby, 1978). One example of such science was the theory of atavism which proposed that due to a process of genetic recombination, disposition toward crime or "lunacy" or other disorders, was revealed in every feature of the person. The body, the mind, and the behavior of the delinquent were considered to be criminal in nature (Platt, 1977). This supported an emerging belief in a criminal class that could be identified, segregated, and controlled. Dugdale's publication, in 1887, of *The Jukes,* a multigenerational study of one family's depravity, did much to advance this notion (Platt, 1977). A more enlightened perspective may recognize these explanations as pseudoscientific, class biased, and a basis for discriminatory policy, but at the time they offered a desired opportunity for action.

In these explanations, it is possible to trace the tracks that lead to more modern justifications for intrusive interventions in the individual and family lives of youthful offenders. Much of the purportedly explanatory content that was historically applied to the urban ethnic poor, has found its way into present day applications centered on the inner-city African-American youth and family.

IMPERATIVES FOR INTERVENTION

As suggested above, early nineteenth century reform efforts were grounded in moral and religious imperatives. The whole notion of child-saving embodied a moral obligation to protect and provide for the most obviously dependent of society's members. Mirroring American concerns from across the Atlantic, in 1851 (Carpenter, 1969, p. 135) a reformer noted that:

> The enormity and amount of juvenile depravity is a subject which now most painfully engages the public mind. These things have long been known to the few: -- now they are made evident to the many: and it is equally clear that if the evil is not checked, it must increase. Now we see, therefore our sin remaineth if we strive not to remove the evil".

During the waning days of the nineteenth century, however, there was increased application, albeit rudimentary, of scientific modes of inquiry. Along with this more secular approach, came an expanded sense of public responsibility. The term "social welfare" was coming into usage as a replacement for the older term of "charities and corrections" (Leiby 1978). The change in terminology reflected a growing sense of the interdependence of people in society, as well as an increased acceptance of the need for government to shoulder responsibility for the welfare of all its citizens.

Philanthropic voluntarism was yielding to the creation of a new technology of social treatment, with various specializations (Leiby, 1978). According to Leiby (1978), the belief systems of Christianity, Liberalism, and Mercantilism, were the driving forces of society which contributed to an unprecedented economic development. The perceived power of these forces, and the realization of substantial wealth on a societal scale, have been linked to the optimistic view of reformers that injustices and inequities could be overturned. The establishment of the Children's Aid Society, the work of the Charity Organization Societies, the beginning of the Settlement movement, and the initiation of the Juvenile Court, each represent unique and significant manifestations of the effort to improve social functioning (Bruno, 1957; Sutton, 1988). The application of material resources, and professionalization and specialization of social welfare service delivery systems, contributed to evolution of large public systems devoted to resolution of particular social problems, including juvenile delinquency.

CHANGING THE CHILD
From 1815 to 1845, there was a burst of support for specialized institutions as the method of choice for treating the various individual disorders which impacted society (Leiby, 1978). An institution offered an attractive means of meeting the need for social control by isolating identified deviants, while providing specialized intervention with individuals, and developing increased knowledge about the particular disorder through focused study (Leiby, 1978). There was a concurrent move toward more humane practices evidenced by the substitution of hard labor for corporal punishment in prisons, the use of educational rather than penal models for children, and the emerging belief that mental illness was due to physiological problems with the brain rather than possession by evil.

Institutions for changing children were referred to initially as Houses of Refuge and later as reformatories, which reflects the primary purpose of reforming the child's character. An activist (Carpenter, 1969, p. 121) outlined operational principles for reformatories as follows:

> [There must be] a strong faith in the immortality of the human soul, the universal and parental government of God, and the equal value in His sight of each of these poor perishing creatures with the most exalted of our race. Love must be the ruling sentiment of all who attempt to influence and guide these children. This love must be wise as well as kind... The reformatory must be a well-managed system, guided by undeviating order and regularity in the whole

school, to which it will be evident that the master is bound as well as the scholars, and for which he will take opportunities of showing them are as necessary for their comfort and well-being as for his. Industrial training should be a part of the school. Personal cleanliness is important...no punishments of a degrading or revengeful nature will ever be employed.

To this, she added that moral training and intellectual growth should also be included. These basic principles laid down in 1851, later expressed with less religious language, have served to characterize the self descriptions of most child-caring institutions for the next century and a half.

In 1869, the chaplain of the New York House of Refuge, which was one of the earliest child-caring institutions, described the aims of the institution as follows (Pierce, 1869, p. 156):

The object of a reformatory is not to send forth a class of highly educated and polished young persons, but to raise up out of the dust, hundreds now festering in sinful homes and vicious societies: to hold them near the truth until their minds shall be impressed with it: to teach them the use of the personal implements with which, in most cases in the humblest walks of life, they will secure an honest living: and then give them a fair start, with hard labor and an honest purpose, to create for themselves a comfortable home.

Two common forms of institutions were the congregate and the cottage plans. The congregate model was used in the establishment of the New York House of Refuge in 1825, and its counterpart in Boston in 1826. The congregate system favored a facility located close to an urban center, with boys housed in large units that were relatively impersonal and highly structured. It was considered an advantage to remain in the urban environment and utilize the industrial resources of the city. Many of the youth were engaged in work that supported the business interests of the large city.

As the century progressed, however, the cottage plan emerged as a favored form for institutions. The cottage plan was well- publicized and succinctly described by juvenile corrections experts. Enoch Wines enunciated the formula that children under the age of fourteen, lacking appropriate guardianship, should come into the care of the state, whereupon they would be placed for an indeterminate period, in institutions with facilities of about forty boys each which were to be located in the country away from the evils of the city, and modeled after the life of an "honest family" (Platt, 1977).

By the very early twentieth century, the methodology of institutional treatment of juvenile delinquency was clarified and refined, and enjoyed international application. Basic principles of this methodology included forfeiture of parental rights when parents demonstrated incompetence (presumably by virtue of the child's arrest); treatment of offenders as juveniles rather than as adults until age eighteen; indefinite sentencing to ensure an adequate period for reformation; use of probation during the post release period; use of the institution as a necessary, but temporary intervention; provision of high quality industrial training to facilitate employment after release; individualized assessment of the character of the inmates as the basis for grouping in cottage units; and sparing use of corporal punishment (Russell & Rigby, 1906).

The period of 1910 to 1920, however, introduced scrutiny of the practice of institutionalization. Several articles appeared in "The Survey", a favorite magazine of social welfare reformers at the time, criticizing operations of the child care institutions and the juvenile court (Coffeen, 1910; Ellwood, 1910; Lattimore, 1910; Lane, 1915; Addition & Deardorff, 1919). Major objections had to do with the juvenile court practice that brought delinquent and dependent children into the same proceedings, and the level of physical care provided to children in the institutions.

A method of changing deviant children that offered an alternative to institutionalization was the controversial practice of "placing out", as championed by C.L. Brace and the Children's Aid Society. Under this program, urban waifs were to be saved from the evils of eastern cities by sending them to the wide open spaces of the western states like Minnesota and Michigan. Thousands of children were "placed out" of the old cities and indentured on farms over a span of several years (Pumphrey & Pumphrey, 1961). It became known, through studies such as that of Hastings H. Hart in 1884, that a great number of children were scattered over several states and transferred from family to family and "...became lost to the knowledge of the state..." which placed them out (Pumphrey & Pumphrey, 1961). The conceptual basis of placing out was that a child would do better in a family environment, with the benefit of hard work and contribution, than in an institution.

CREATION OF THE JUVENILE COURT
The establishment of the first Juvenile Courts in Illinois and Colorado in 1899, significantly expanded the reach of government into the private lives of children and families. It has been noted that the "juvenile justice system", prior to the genesis of the Juvenile Court was a very diverse and loose collection of private and public institutions and community programs that were served by the civil court (Ferdinand, 1991). The authority of the civil court, while respected in the field, was informal, and provided very little control over the staffing, budgets, practice, or objectives of the programs it fed (Ferdinand, 1991).

The creation of the Juvenile Court represents a concentration of authority with the aim of matching children and appropriate interventions (Sutton, 1988). With such a mission, the Juvenile Court took on responsibility for all youthful offenders, and established itself as the central decision-making entity for all matters pertaining to the disposition of juvenile delinquents, including removal from the family home.

MODERN PRACTICE APPROACHES
Although the fundamental form of cottage plan institutions has been maintained throughout the twentieth century, adjunctive components and alternative approaches have been applied (Young, Dore, & Pappenfort, 1986). These include the addition of highly structured group homes in community settings, and the integration of family involvement and family therapy models in institutional milieus, as well as intensive in-home services, multi-systemic treatment, boot camps, balanced and restorative justice conferences, and use of a correctional model.

This brief discussion of modern practice approaches is presented to highlight the additions and alternatives to confinement that have been attempted in recent years. It is offered to counter the impression that out-of-home placement is the only available alternative for intervention in juvenile delinquency.

Residential care, although not significantly changed in basic structure, exhibits notable shifts along dimensions of agency size and auspices, and complexity of services, from the mid-1960's into the early 1980's (Young, Dore, & Pappenfort, 1986). A trend toward smaller private agencies with greater functional complexity in service of delinquent youth has been observed. Modern delinquency treatment practices have continued to include relatively traditional institutional programs, which incorporate greater emphasis on group treatment modalities and an "aftercare" component, which attempts to follow youth back into their home communities.

During the late 1970's and into the early 1990's, increasing application of ecological principles in the formulation of innovative treatment approaches occurred. The community-based movement of the 1970's brought the proliferation of smaller group homes established in neighborhoods (Young, Dore, & Pappenfort 1986). The 1980's and 1990's were characterized by rapid development of family focused programming based on systems theory concepts and family therapy approaches. In more recent years, however, there has been a counteracting influence that leads to implementation of correctional rather than treatment models. These practice approaches are explicated below.

Family Involvement
Due to clinical experience and rudimentary program evaluation efforts, it was widely accepted in the residential care field in the 1970's that treatment outcomes for delinquent youth could be improved with greater attention to family interactions and community based interventions (Coughlin, Maloney, Baron, Dahir, Daly, Daly, Fixen, Phillips, & Thomas, 1982). The treatment literature espoused the advantages of "family involvement" in residential treatment programs (Colon, 1981; Krona, 1980; Whittaker, 1979). Such efforts included family education regarding the systemic nature of delinquent behaviors, attempts to raise the frequency and quality of family functioning, and experiments with inclusion of the family alternatively as part of the treatment team, or as the primary client. In practice, such efforts yielded numerous and costly administrative issues, but raised consciousness of family interactions and paved the way for incorporation of family therapy models into the residential milieu. This

process of integration of family and existing residential models has been described as a developmental process which encompassed grand scale shifts in attitudes, resources, and agency policies (McConkey-Radetzki, 1986). In order to smooth this transition, some agencies incorporated sophisticated computerized clinical information systems and complimentary staff development programs (Mooradian & Grasso, 1993).

Family Therapy
While outcome studies of family therapy approaches with delinquents are generally confounded by the conduct of family therapy along with other treatment components in residential settings, they are also subject to some notable conceptual and methodological difficulties. In a review of general family therapy research, Bednar, Burlingame, and Masters (1988) noted the conclusion that the family behavioral therapies are found to be as effective as other psychotherapies, but added their observation that rigorous research was limited by a lack of semantic and measurement precision.

Shadish, Montgomery, Wilson, Bright, and Okumabua (1993), conducted a meta-analysis of family therapy outcome studies published from 1963 to 1988, and found an effect size of .53 ($n = 16$) for conduct disorder and delinquency treatment. Chamberlain and Rosicky (1995), conducted a subsequent meta-analysis of studies from 1988 to 1994 that specifically addressed family therapy for conduct disorder and delinquency. By using a selection strategy that combined research rigor and therapy specification, they were able to analyze studies that escaped the criticism of earlier reviewers, and found that family therapy significantly improved outcomes as compared to individual or group treatment alone. They further noted that family therapy significantly increased the likelihood that youth would either remain with, or return to, their own family after confinement. Nelson (1990) found that family focused programs were successful at preventing out-of-home placement for status offenders and other delinquents at the significantly high rates of 67% to 100%, and 50% to 90%, respectively.

Another variation on Structural and Strategic family therapy (called Brief Strategic Family Therapy) has been described by Robins and Szapocznik (2000). This program was developed in a venue that services a primarily Latino population, and focuses on youth between the ages of 8 and 17 who are either already displaying, or at-risk for behavior problems, including substance abuse. The program was instituted to prevent and decrease delinquent behavior. Techniques of Structural Family Therapy, including restructuring family relationships, and improving interaction with the environment are utilized over the course of 12-15 sessions for a duration of about 3 months. While no outcome research is cited by Robbins and Szapocznik (2000) they summarize prior research that supported the superiority of Structural Family Therapy approaches over individual Psychodynamic therapy and group treatment.

Intensive In-Home Services
Intensive in-home family service programs are heavily connected to the family preservation movement that grew out of the foster care arena (Woods, 1988). The advent of "permanency planning" as a way to prevent serial foster care placements gave rise to the popularity of attempts to maintain young people in their family homes (Maluccio & Fein, 2002).

These programs seek to prevent out-of-home placement of youth, by committing relatively high levels of resources to the family of the youth for strictly limited periods (Woods, 1988). Philosophically, they are rooted in a speech presented in 1912 by Judge Julian Mack of Chicago, who posed an interrogative regarding why the state would not assign the same amount of money invested in out-of-home placement to the support of families with wayward youth (Whittaker, 2002). The essential components of family preservation practice include the belief that the family is the ideal developmental context for the child; the notion that services should be first and foremost supportive and strengthening of the family; the provision of services that are culturally sensitive and strength-based; and utilization of an ecological perspective which facilitates changing environments as well as individual and family functioning (Whittaker, 2002). Such programs are based on an amalgamation of theories including crisis intervention, family systems, social learning, and human ecology (Barth, 1989).

The most widely applied model of intensive in-home family treatment is the Homebuilders program (Kinney, Haapala, Booth, & Leavitt, 1989). Homebuilders workers are available to their client families at any time during the four to six weeks of treatment. They work with two to four families at any given time. Limited goals are established with the family and evaluated weekly. Although originally intended to serve child welfare cases, the Homebuilders model gained appeal due to claims of high success rates in preventing out-of-home placement, and by emphasizing cost savings. In Michigan, the model was instituted as the Families First program for child welfare cases, and was eventually expanded to serve delinquency cases (OCYS, 1988). Although internal program evaluation efforts claimed extremely high rates of success, defined as no out-of-home placement at three months after intervention, no independent studies of effectiveness have been located.

A Family Empowerment Intervention (FEI) has been described by Dembo, Dudell, Livingston, and Schmeidler (2001). This approach maintains the offending youth in the family home and applies concentrated resources to strengthen the family. It involves the use of Structural Family Therapy, ecological systems interventions, and transgenerational family therapy. Service is provided by "highly trained non-professionals" who serve as "Field Consultants", with contacts occurring a minimum of three times per week for a maximum of ten weeks. Effectiveness of FEI has been evaluated by its developers (Dembo, Ramirez-Garcia, Schmeidler, Rollie, Livingston, & Hartsfield, 2001). They found that youth whose families had received the FEI experienced significantly fewer arrests (mean -.17) and fewer charges (mean -.25) at twelve months post intervention when compared to youth whose families did not receive the FEI.

Another common intervention is Intensive Supervision or In-Home Detention. These interventions seek to provide external control over the delinquent without physical confinement (Barton & Butts, 1990). Control measures range from unpredictable contact with a supervision worker through electronic tethering. In a study designed to test the efficacy of these programs as an alternative to state wardship (which is a reasonable proxy for placement in traditional programs), Barton and Butts (1990) followed, for two years, a primarily inner-city African-American sample of 500 youth who were randomly assigned to one of three experimental intensive supervision programs, and a control group. Their findings indicate that the intensive supervision programs successfully graduated 46% of assigned youth. The remainder were terminated due to a lack of behavioral progress. These graduates were compared to the control group. The mean number of charges filed against program youth was 2.63, while it was only 1.31 for the control group. The investigators, however, reasoned that the program youth were "at large" for longer periods of time (18.3 months for program youth and only 10.68 months for control youth), and so had a longer period of exposure to opportunities for recidivism. In an attempt to equalize this discrepancy, they constructed an index to produce a "mean number of weighted criminal charges" that allowed them to compare program youth more favorably to control youth. This weighted average was 3.69 versus 3.58 for the groups respectively, and the difference was not significant. Although the authors conclude that intensive supervision is a viable alternative to traditional wardship, their research appears to align data with a preferred conclusion.

Multi-Systemic Treatment

Multi-Systemic treatment (MST) of serious and violent offenders is based on the assumption that adolescent behavior is embedded in complex and interconnected systems involving individual, peer, family, school, and community levels (Henggeler, 1991). Treatment intervention is directed at each of these levels, as well as their interfaces. MST utilizes case management, educational interventions, family therapy, and supportive interventions known as "nurturing" or "mentoring".

Sutphen, Thyer, and Kurtz (1995) implemented the model with 80 "high risk" juvenile offenders and found significant improvements in family relationships, life skills, school performance, peer relationships, and delinquent behavior. Bourduin (1995) tested the model for effectiveness in comparison with individual treatment.

With a sample of 176 juvenile offenders identified as being at high risk for committing additional serious crimes, he found MST to be more effective in improving key family correlates of antisocial behavior and in ameliorating adjustment problems in individual youth. He also compared four-year re-arrest rates and found MST to be more effective in preventing future criminal behavior in comparison to individual treatment.

Henggler, Melton, and Smith, (1992) cast MST as a form of family preservation, and conducted a rigorous comparison of MST and out-of-home delinquency placement. This study used a sample of 84 serious offenders who were randomly assigned to each of the treatment conditions. A pretest/posttest format was used to compare the youth on several variables, including family relationships, peer relationships, psychiatric symptomatology, social competence, and self-reported delinquency. The investigators found no significant differences among the demographic and psychosocial variables, but a check of archival records one year later indicated that the MST youth showed significantly fewer arrests as well as self-reported offenses. Curiously, they also reported that the MST youth were confined an average of ten fewer weeks than those in the Youth Services group. This may lead a reader to question the efficacy of MST as a family preservation intervention, since the goal of such programs is to totally prevent removal of the youth from the family home. Also raised by this study are questions regarding the specific effects of MST on the other variables that may represent its goals. Nonetheless, it appears that MST functions as an ecological intervention, and is reasonably effective when compared to traditional out-of-home placement. Such knowledge also supports the value of an ecological approach to intervention with serious delinquents.

Henggeler (1997) also notes several other field studies using MST with juvenile offenders and summarizes similar findings. These interventions have been delivered in South Carolina, Missouri, and Tennessee.

Boot Camps

Growing out of enchantment with the "Scared Straight" initiative in the 1970's, boot camps gained popularity in the 1990's. Although the effectiveness of "Scared Straight" programs, which used intensive verbal confrontation by prison inmates to deter youthful offenders, has been effectively challenged, a notion that various forms of intimidation can change delinquent behavior continues to persist (Petrosino, Turpin-Petrosino, & Finckenauer, 2000).

Boot camps, which are sometimes referred to as "shock camps", offered proponents a similarly enchanting option. Boot camps have been developed to protect the public, reduce crowding in juvenile detention and residential facilities, reduce costs of intervention when compared to traditional residential facilities, hold offenders accountable, deter future crime, and rehabilitate offenders (Cronin,

1994). Boot camps typically remove youth from their home and community for a relatively short duration (from one weekend to ninety days), whereas traditional residential care lasts from six months to over a year. The short-term residential component of boot camp programs is usually supplemented with an "aftercare" component that involves continued work with the youth in his or her home community. The residential phase of boot camp programs generally uses interventions that mirror military techniques from basic training, to mold new behavior and thinking patterns for the youth.

Research evaluating the effect of boot camps shows mixed results. Peters, Thomas, and Zamberlin (1997) found advantages in the use of boot camps, including typically lower per diem costs for the residential component compared to traditional residential treatment programs. In their study, recidivism rates for youth released from boot camps were compared to those for youth involved in three traditional programs. Recidivism rates were "comparable" to traditional programs for two of the boot camps, but significantly higher for one program. In addition, for youth who re-offended, the boot camp youth did so much sooner after release than did the traditional program youth. These results indicate that boot camp interventions may be helpful for some youthful offenders, but not for many others.

In research focused on young offenders after boot camp intervention, Stinchcomb and Terry (2001) found that boot camps do not significantly impact re-arrest rates. They found, further, that race (being African-American) was the best predictor of re-arrest, with significant effects provided by type of release, prior felony history, and age.

In addition, Benda, Toombs, and Peacock (2002, p. 65) concluded that there is "no consistent evidence of the effectiveness of boot camp programs in reducing drug use or criminal recidivism" by young offenders. In their research, a sophisticated "survival analysis" technique was used to examine the "time to recidivism" for young adult offenders who were released from boot camp programs three years prior. For their sample of 480 males aged 16-40 (that was 42% European-American and 45% African-American) 58% of the former boot camp residents returned to the Department of Corrections within three years. A notable factor in successfully predicting non-recidivism was the expectation by the offender that the boot camp program would provide him with valuable benefits.

Balanced and Restorative Justice Conferences

Balanced and restorative justice is a concept that involves equal regard for the victim of crime and the offender. It seeks to replace traditional juvenile justice issues regarding who is responsible, what law was broken, and what should be done to punish the offender, with alternatives. These include identification of the nature of harm, what needs to be done to "make it right" or repair the harm, and who is responsible for this repair (Zehr, 1990). Balanced and restorative justice is a framework that seeks to engage victims, offenders and their families, and members of the community as resources in an effective response to crime (Bazemore & Umbreit, 2001).

Balanced and restorative justice conferences involve a facilitated and structured face-to-face meeting of victim and offender. During such a conference, the victim and others describe how they have been affected and may question the offender. The offender responds, and typically apologizes for the behavior. At the end of the conference, the participants formally agree on ways in which restitution can be made, and other requirements such as community service or improvement in school are established for the offender.

This approach has been used with youthful offenders in Australia, New Zealand, and various cities in the United States (McGarrell, 2001). A randomized study compared the use of balanced and restorative justice conferences to traditional court processing with 458 early offenders who were less than age 14 and had no prior adjudications (McGarrell, 2001). Re-arrest rates at six months and twelve months after intervention were significantly lower for the balanced and restorative justice youth than for the court-processed youth. These findings indicate the promise that the approach may hold for intervention with less serious offenders.

Correctional Model

Howell (1998) points out that juvenile justice approaches appear to be completing a cycle. The first major reform effort separated juveniles from adult offenders and gave rise to the specialized institution. The second phase began with formation of the juvenile court and provided the legal basis for a more extensive and cohesive system. The third began in the mid-twentieth century with a focus on prevention and diversion from traditional placements. A fourth era seems to be underway wherein there is a call for once again adjudicating youth as adults. There are numerous and vocal proponents of a "get tough" approach that opposes traditional protection and treatment for delinquent youth (Howell 1998). The trend toward treating juveniles as adult offenders has been enacted in state statutes. By 1997, 14 states had enacted some form of mandatory waiver of juveniles to adult court (Butts & Mitchell, 2000). Indiana legislators, for example, passed a law that required the juvenile court to waive any juvenile offender with a prior adjudication, who is charged with a felony, regardless of the youth's age.

Despite empirical identification of pockets of opinion that maintain support for a rehabilitative ideal, many observers have noted a strain of sentiment that favors more punitive interventions (Moon, Sundt, Cullen, & Wright, 2000). On one hand, liberals attacked the operation of the juvenile justice system on the grounds that it abused the principles of the juvenile's right to treatment by denying due process protections and establishing arbitrary judgments and controls in the name of individualized treatment. On the other hand, conservatives agreed that the juvenile justice system was flawed, but argued that the flaws led to ineffective treatment of juvenile offenders and inadequate protection of society (Moon, Sundt, Cullen, & Wright, 2000).

In concert with a conservative political climate and increased public fear of violent youth, has come what may be termed the correctional model for intervention in juvenile delinquency. It carries an emphasis on community protection rather than individual rehabilitation. Proponents of the correctional model favor lowered age limits for trial with adult status, specific sentences for identified felonies, increased discretionary powers of county prosecutors, and trading treatment dollars for increasingly secure facilities. The State of Michigan, for example, conducted a $37.6 million project involving removal of existing treatment cottage facilities and replacement with high security buildings and perimeter reinforcements at the large W.J. Maxey Boys' Training School near Detroit (Oppat, 1998). This facility was previously operated as an "open" group-oriented treatment "campus" for most of Michigan's serious juvenile offenders since the late 1960's.

It was supplemented with the maximum security Green Oak Center, which services approximately one-fourth the population of the open program. With this development, it appears that the differences in structure and objective between the two facilities are rapidly dissolving.

MODERN POLICY ISSUES

The doctrine of *parens patriae*, which serves as the legal cornerstone of Juvenile Court proceedings, was challenged by reformers in the 1990's (Ferdinand, 1991). As the foundation for a system that allows the state to act in place of parents (*in loco parentis*), the doctrine has been interpreted as an "either/or" principle, wherein children are considered to be either the responsibility of the parents, or that of the state (Weiss, 1990). Responsibility for children has been traditionally transferred from parents to government only when families fail to provide adequate control. Such a condition requires that parents be found incompetent in order for the child to be processed and placed into treatment. Such a system creates adversity between the family and treatment providers and tends to favor out-of-home placement. It has been suggested that an alternative, based on joint and interdependent responsibility of the family, community, and state might prove to be more effective. Support for this alternative is provided in the separate reports of five distinct commissions which studied the juvenile justice system (Weiss, 1990). Proponents of such an approach characterize it as family-centered as opposed to child-centered or bureaucracy-centered. This collaborative approach is gaining strength and is favored by some Juvenile Court judges, but is far from being fully implemented (Hatchett, 1998). Parental rights continue to be compromised, and huge numbers of juveniles are placed out of their family homes each year (Weiss, 1990).

Status as a juvenile, and acceptance of the ideal that youthful offenders have a "right to treatment", have produced several compromises to the due process protections that would otherwise be afforded those subjected to confinement (Ferdinand, 1991). Reliance on recommendations of caseworkers in court proceedings, indeterminate sentencing, broad discretionary powers of staff in detention and treatment facilities, and informal assessments all may have eroded the protections available to juveniles. While the stated motivations have always been to act in the best interest of the child, a paternalistic discretionary system allows greater likelihood of arbitrary dispositions. Paradoxically, an interest in saving children may actually subject them to greater intrusions on personal freedom than are experienced by adult offenders.

Some observers have raised concerns with forms of confinement in other venues such as the use of private psychiatric hospitals for delinquent behaviors (Eamon, 1994). Such use may further circumvent the requirements for due process established for juveniles processed through normal juvenile justice channels. Extending this area of concern, Johnson (1996) suggests that even broader forms of social control exist for delinquents and their families. Under the concept of "transcarceration", he includes the use of educational systems and welfare systems as modes of social control. While it may be argued that such an extension of the concept of government intrusion (and the need for due process protection) may be excessive, Johnson's notion effectively raises consciousness of additional means of social control, particularly as they apply to low-income African-Americans.

One alternative to the "right to treatment" doctrine is application of a "just desserts" model. This approach asserts that it is no longer appropriate to consider all juveniles as dependent and in need of the protection of the state (Ashford, 1988). It favors more formalized decision-making about placement based on community risk, lowered age limits for trial with adult status, increased discretion for prosecutors, and reduced numbers of offenders placed in juvenile treatment facilities.

EMERGENT THEORIES OF DELINQUENCY
The following theories outline current constructions of the factors that are thought to contribute to delinquent behavior, and presumably lead to subsequent confinements.

Strain Theory
Strain theory holds that delinquency flows from frustration due to interference with goal-directed behavior and an incongruence of values and opportunity. It is primarily sociological in orientation and focuses on the impact of individual and community interaction. Applied to the particular experience of many African-American youth, this theory may

be helpful in locating the impact of oppressive opportunity structures, peer influences, and limited availability of adult males.

Classic strain theory has been presented in the work of Merton (1938), Cohen (1955), and Cloward and Ohlin (1960). These explanations are characterized by a focus on the inability of adolescents to attain long-range economic or status goals through socially legitimated processes. The image of delinquency that emerges from this branch of theory is one of the urban youth from a disenfranchised ethnic or racial group, who is systematically denied opportunities for advancement due to discriminatory practices and capitalistic motivations.

Newer versions of strain theory (Elliot & Voss, 1974; Greenberg, 1977; Empey, 1985) replace the blockage of long-range goals with a focus on more immediate social goals such as popularity with peers, academic success, athletic achievement, and developing reasonable relationships with significant adults. Success in achieving these types of goals may vary on a daily basis, so greater variability in delinquent behavior is anticipated when compared to the earlier formulation of strain theory.

A further updated version of strain theory includes the role of blockage from avoidance of painful or aversive events (Agnew, 1985). The rationale in this case states that inability to employ legitimated paths of avoidance of unpleasant life circumstances may lead to the selection of illegal escape attempts.

Sub-Cultural Deviance Theory

According to this branch of theory, it is association with negative peers that is central to the development of delinquent behavior. The peer group is defined as a subculture. A tenet in original formulations of this theory is that association with delinquent others leads to acceptance of delinquent values, which in turn leads to delinquent behavior (Agnew, 1992). Working from a recognition of mechanisms other than the infusion of delinquent values, Briar and Piliavin (1965) assert that youth may commit delinquent acts in an effort to prove their courage or remain loyal to peers. Similarly, Short and Strodbeck (1963) look to the significance of maintaining or enhancing status within the peer group as a cause of delinquent behavior. If peer group norms support antisocial behavior, then those norms will be reinforced, in opposition to the values of larger social systems, through personal interactions within the subculture. Johnson, Marcos, and Bohr (1987) explained delinquent behavior, in the form of drug use, through the situational pressures applied by peers.

From this perspective, group membership, belonging, and individual identity emerge as factors to be considered in investigation of delinquent behavior and multiple confinements. Once a youth is labeled "delinquent" and coercively grouped with other "delinquents", existing problems with personal associations and identity may be exacerbated. Such a process holds special implications for youth caught in a cycle of multiple confinements.

Rational Choice Theory

Rational Choice Theory rests upon the idea that offenders seek personal benefit or gain through delinquent behavior. Cornish and Clarke (1986) point out that the delinquent makes choices about behavior, and decides to engage in activities that provide some form of economic or psychic reward. This reward may be material or mental. They characterize this process as a rational one, but acknowledge that it is limited by the situation and predisposition of the individual in question.

The desire to obtain personal rewards within an environment that disallows socially supported avenues, may explain delinquency and subsequent confinement. Money or excitement may be the desired outcomes of delinquent behavior, and, from this perspective, the delinquent youth is one who deliberately decides to obtain them through illegal means. Although a greater emphasis is placed on personal decision-making in Rational Choice Theory, it is similar to Strain Theory in its implication of opportunity structures in the production and maintenance of delinquent behavior.

Social Control Theory

Social Control Theory holds that adolescents who function without the benefit of effective structure and accountability measures engage in delinquent activities. This branch of theory may be related to the development of impulse control or internalization of prosocial values (Nye 1958). In this regard, authors have focused on the complementary roles of attachment or cohesion and discipline functions within families. Nye (1958) dealt with the contribution of direct controls which he viewed as the immediate application or threat of punishments and rewards to gain compliance with social norms.   Nye also recognized that the impact of direct controls would be limited outside the physical proximity of parents, and raised the importance of the psychological presence of the parent as a deterrent to antisocial behavior.   Wells and Rankin (1988) were influential in defining components of direct controls, including specification of acceptable behaviors, monitoring of youthful activity, and application of discipline.

Bahr (1979) recognized the utility of the concept of attachment between parent and child as an explanatory mechanism for adolescent motivation to conform.   Research has supported the idea that parental discipline is more effective in reducing adolescent noncompliance within the context of high parent-child attachment (Wells & Rankin, 1988).   Eron, Walder, and Lefkowitz (1971) found that punishment of boys who were not strongly attached to their parents seemed to instigate aggressive behaviors.

Social Control Theory centers on the role of parental behaviors and family interaction in the production and maintenance of delinquent behavior.   These assertions overlap with conclusions drawn from the literature on family functioning, and provide a useful basis for construction of the models investigated in this book.

These four theories of delinquency emphasize various subsystems of the youth's social ecology.   Together, they cover a spectrum of possible factors that are hypothesized to contribute to delinquent behavior.   The next chapter reviews empirical knowledge about the links between some of these theoretical factors and delinquency.

CHAPTER 4

Social Ecology and Delinquency

This book is grounded in an ecological framework, which is used to build understanding of the complex problem of disproportionate minority confinement. The ecological perspective posits that human beings act in the context of multiple systems. These systems are interrelated and hierarchically arranged. At the largest levels, they include the natural environment, the human-constructed environment, and the social-behavioral environment (Kilsdonk, 1983). Social systems have also been conceptualized as occupying four levels of proximity to individual persons (Bronfrenbrenner, 1979). In distal order, they include the micro, meso, exo, and macro levels. Micro-systems are those that most closely surround the individual, including the home and the school. Meso-systems are those that establish the interactions between micro-environments, such as the neighborhood and parent-teacher conferences. Exo-systems include those entities that create a context for meso-systems, such as local government or employment opportunities. Macro-systems operate at the most distant level from the individual, but establish rules and boundaries for interaction and personal experience. They include large organizations such as national governments, meaning-making systems such as culture, and ideologies such as capitalism or racism. From the ecological perspective, individuals and families operate in transaction with their respective environmental systems. In this context, the term transaction means that the individual and the environment interact reciprocally, and that both are changed through each sequence of interaction (Germain & Bloom, 1999). Such a view inextricably links person and environment in each behavioral event. This linkage not only establishes opportunities for empowerment of individuals, but also facilitates understanding of the impact of environmental influences on individual functioning.

The ecological perspective can be used to inform selection of relevant variables when studying a complicated personal-social problem such as disproportionate minority confinement. It may also provide a basis for balancing the attribution of individual and societal responsibility for juvenile delinquency.

In accord with this ecological orientation, it is instructive to consider two additional areas of the literature as a means of locating the work documented in this book within the context of existing knowledge. They include the relationship of stress and coping to delinquency, and the relationship of family functioning to delinquency. Stress and coping responses have been identified as contributors to behavioral and mental health problems including delinquency, especially for minority youth. Aspects of limited family functioning have been implicated in the development of delinquent activity for all youth.

Both stress and coping, and family functioning represent examples of linkages of person and environment that specifically relate to juvenile delinquency. The literature review that follows is presented to illuminate the transactions that are experienced by many African-American delinquent youth.

THE RELATIONSHIP OF STRESS AND COPING TO DELINQUENCY

The type, duration, and intensity of stress, along with the youth's chosen means of coping, have been identified as factors that are related to delinquent behavior (McCubbin, Kapp, & Thompson, 1993; Stiffman, Dore, & Cunningham, 1996; Spaccarelli, 1997). A review of the stress and coping literature provides a basis for inclusion of these variables in the analysis conducted here, and grounds construction of the multiple regression models that are used to address the research questions identified for the present study.

Conceptual Issues Regarding Stress and Coping

Stress and coping occupy deep space in the clinical literature. Although several models of stress and coping have been advanced, it is instructive to review one such model that is representative of modern conceptualizations in the field. Millgram (1989) points out that the term "stress" has suffered from diverse application and ambiguous definition. Two decades earlier, stress was commonly defined as any change in one's environment that elicits a high degreeof emotional tension which interferes with normal patterns of response, and that requires behavioral adaptation. Millgram offers an alternative that views stress as an "imbalance between stimulus demand and response supply" (1989, p 401). In this manner, stress is redefined as an interactive process of the person and environment. Stressful events are referred to as "stressors" and responses are seen as "stress mediating variables". Possible responses are stress reactions (transient maladaptive behaviors), stress disorders (crystallized clinical syndromes), and coping. Adaptive attempts to mediate stress are referred to as coping, which is based on cognitive appraisal of available intrapersonal and social resources, and may take the form of problem-focused or emotion-focused coping behaviors. Millgram (1989) allows for "objective" and "subjective" appraisals of the level of loss and personal responsibility associated with a particular stressor, and acknowledges the important role of the personal meaning attached to an event.

A complement to Millgram's conception of stress as an imbalance comes from the sociological literature on mental health. Pearlin (1989) suggests that the structural arrangements within which individuals are embedded determine the stressors they encounter, the stress mediators they are able to mobilize, and their inner experiences of stress. Such a conceptualization locates social statuses such as age, gender, and race as independent variables. From this perspective, other investigators have concluded that stress is an intervening variable between social status and psychological functioning (Aneshensel, Rutter, & Lachenbruch, 1991). In other words, social position organizes the sources of stress encountered, and methods of coping available for a given individual, and shapes psychological adaptation. This framework offers advantages for those interested in disproportionate minority confinement in its recognition of ecological influences. Such an approach has received support from other researchers (Turner, Wheaton, & Lloyd, 1995). A further extension of this branch of thinking is provided by Rosella (1993) who highlighted the role of "disadvantaged social contexts" in placing low-income black youth at risk for physical and mental health difficulties including depression and delinquency. In this manner, the combined effects of poverty and race may be seen as a social status that exerts powerful impacts on mental health and other behavioral outcomes. This conception of stress and coping may illuminate the ecology of young African-American males, in highly pressurized environments such as urban areas.

Research on Stress and Coping Related to Delinquency

Much practice experience has indicated that children of divorce, violence, alcoholism, and incest have been highly represented in adult clinical populations. Therefore, researchers in the 1970's and 1980's focused on the development of statistical risk models and found that stress factors such as poverty, neighborhood violence, parental absence, and employment instability, increased the likelihood that children would become delinquent, drug-addicted, or chronic mental health cases (Butler, 1997).

Some researchers have focused specifically on delinquency as an outcome variable and attempted to investigate the relative roles that stress and coping have played in the onset of delinquent behavior (McCubbin, Kapp, & Thompson, 1993; Stiffman, Dore, & Cunningham, 1996; Spaccarelli, 1997). Two tracks of such research are considered below. One attempts to establish a linkage of stress to the production of delinquency, and the other searches for the more specific relationships of particular stressors and coping strategies to delinquent behaviors.

Among the first category of studies is that of Vaux and Ruggiero (1983). Their study was one of the earliest published attempts to employ a retrospective design and correlational approach to determine whether there was a significant association between life stress and delinquency. Regression analysis indicated that life changes added significantly to age and socio-economic status in predicting violence, theft, drug use, and property damage for their sample. Due to their careful definition of delinquency and adequate measurement of life stress, as well as the inclusion of a non-institutional group of subjects, this study did much to advance understanding of the relationship among these variables.

A more recent example of the same approach is provided by Deutsch (1989). This study used a similar design to determine that under-socialized youth had experienced a greater number of stressful events during their early lives than had their more socialized peers.

In an attempt to build knowledge of both stress and coping in relation to delinquency, Hoffman and Su (1997) investigated potential gender differences. They noted that the general stress literature identified gender as a mediator of stress and adjustment, but investigated potential differences between males and females. Theyconcluded that for their delinquent sample, stressful events exert a similar short-term impact on both adolescent males and females.

Some studies have investigated specific linkages of stressors and favored coping strategies within selected groups of troubled youth. Utilizing an apparently all female sample, de Anda, Javidi, Jefford, Komorowski, and Yanez (1991) investigated potential differences in stressors faced and coping employed among groups of pregnant and non-pregnant substance abusing adolescents. Although high levels of exposure to stress were reported by both groups, the only significant difference in types of stressors was the greater role of family members as sources of stress for the substance abusing youth. It was also noted that the pregnant sub-sample indicated a high use of "adaptive" coping strategies such as cognitive control, affective release, and relaxation, while the substance-abusing group used "maladaptive" strategies such as behavioral excess, substance abuse, denial, and withdrawal. Although this study is not directly related to male delinquents, it provides the finding that youth who engage in a particular socially devalued behavior may also display group similarities in coping patterns.

Focusing on a sample of confined delinquents with a history of serious offenses, Burton, Foy, Bwanusi, and Johnson (1994) found that juvenile delinquents are a high risk group for exposure to trauma and the development of stress-related symptomatology. The wording of this conclusion is important in that there is a recognition of the limitations of the retrospective design in attribution of causality. With this design, it is not possible to accurately conclude that trauma and stress lead to delinquency, but it is possible to note that these conditions co-occur. These findings also illustrate the limitations imposed on understanding the effects of systemic feedback by a purely correlational approach because there is no way to express the relative degrees of reciprocal influence. Nonetheless, this study provides evidence for the conclusion that stress and delinquent activity demonstrate an empirical connection.

A retrospective design was also used by Steiner, Garcia, and Matthews (1997). They utilized multiple forms of data collection and a non-clinical age and gender matched comparison group to investigate relationships between Post Traumatic Stress Disorder (PTSD) and delinquency. Thirty-two percent of their delinquent sample met full diagnostic criteria for PTSD, and an additional twenty percent met partial criteria. One-half of the sample indicated that the experienced traumatic event involved witnessing interpersonal violence. The sample also experienced significantly higher levels of distress, anxiety, and depression, and lowered impulse control and suppression of aggression, in contrast to the comparison group.

Further establishing the connections between specific stressors, coping strategies, and behavioral adjustment for delinquents, is the work of Spaccarelli (1997). With a sample of violent delinquents and a low-violence comparison group, it was determined that greater exposure to serious physical abuse and domestic violence involving weapons, and greater use of aggressive control-seeking behaviors in response to stress, were evident for the violent delinquent group. While causation of delinquency cannot be attributed to this exposure, it may be useful to note the commonality of this experience among delinquent youth.

In a longitudinal examination of the linkages between particular stressors and the emergence of violent behavior in adolescents, it was found that almost a third of the variance in violent behaviors could be predicted by a combination of personal variables and environmental variables (Stiffman, Dore, & Cunningham, 1996). Such findings help establish the relevance of an ecological approach which accounts for multilevel variables. This study carries the strengths of using a large inner-city sample with seventy percent African-American participants, repeated interview data collection techniques, multiple geographic sites, and an eight-year time span with four waves of analysis. Specific environmental stressors found to be significantly related to violent behaviors include high community unemployment rates, history of physical abuse, and having mentally ill family members. In addition, an unspecified group of "stressful events" (as contrasted with "traumatic events") was an environmental variable that retained significant predictive value across all four waves. While the resultant article does not provide sufficient information to clarify the operational definition of "stressful events", it does provide confirmation for the connection of stress to the production of violent behaviors in African-American adolescents.

In a study undertaken with youth in residential treatment for delinquency, several specific findings regarding the relationship of coping and adjustment in the forms of program completion and post-placement success were obtained (McCubbin, Kapp, & Thompson, 1993). Youth who primarily utilized professional support, spiritual support, and low activity coping strategies were significantly more likely to successfully complete a group treatment program with a family therapy component, and to do better upon release to the community than did those who used other coping strategies. By contrast, youth who used ventilation (e.g. swearing and open expression of anger), friendship support (e.g. being close with a friend or boy/girlfriend), relaxation (e.g. daydreaming and listening to music), and family problem-solving (e.g. talking with family members and doing things with the family) had greater difficulty completing treatment goals and adjusting to the community after release from the program. These results are carefully interpreted to mean that the fit between the youth's coping behavior and the expectations of the program are critical to success, rather than to say that certain coping strategies are generally more successful for delinquent youth regardless of their environment. Such a finding highlights the role of program structure in successful completion, but leaves open the question of the relationship between successful program completion and post-release adjustment.

A similar study was conducted to increase understanding of the relationship of encounters with stressors and application of coping strategies with residential program completion and post-release adjustment among African-American delinquents (McCubbin, Flemming, Thompson, Neitman, Elver, & Savas, 1995). This study used adaptations of a common coping inventory to determine that change in use of coping strategies over the course of residential treatment was a significant predictor of both program completion and post-release adjustment among samples of African-American male and female delinquents. Specifically, reduction in undesirable youth coping such as "Incendiary Communication and Tension Management", accurately predicted about 69% of program completions. Increases in desirable youth coping such as increased use of "Spiritual and Personal Development", and "Positive Appraisal and Problem Solving", accurately predicted about 75% of program completions among the youth sampled. Focusing on a "less restrictive" living situation at three months post-release, these researchers were able to accurately predict about 65% of post-release living situations with reduction in the undesirable coping strategies listed above. Changes in desirable coping strategies accurately predicted about 73% of post-release living situations. At 12 months post-release, the findings showed about 70% accuracy for predictions of less restrictive living situations based on changes in undesirable youth coping, and 63% to 70% for predictions based on changes in desirable youth coping strategies. Moreover, changes in parental coping strategies were also found to positively impact discriminant analysis of program completion and of post-release living situation. These findings indicate that certain types of coping strategies used by African-American delinquents, and their caregivers, improve the youth's chances of completing the program and entering a post-release living situation in a less-restrictive setting. It is relevant to note that this study contributes to the understanding of what it takes for a young African-American male to be released from an out-of-home a placement. Also, however, it is important to know that a "less restrictive placement" may still be an additional out-of-home placement.

Taken together, this body of research provides support for the conclusion that stressors and coping strategies are significantly associated with the development and maintenance of a broad range of delinquent behaviors, as well as the response of decision-makers within the juvenile justice system. Moreover, these relationships have been demonstrated for males and females, and for African-American and European-American youth. In this way, knowledge about the sources of stress encountered and the forms of coping employed by an adolescent may provide a useful basis for understanding the youth's entry into the juvenile justice system and subsequent out-of-home placement.

THE RELATIONSHIP OF FAMILY FUNCTIONING TO DELINQUENCY

Below, the contributions of family theory and research to understanding disproportionate minority confinement are considered. The brief review of selected aspects of family theory is presented to provide the reader with a foundation in family measurement models as they apply to delinquency. The review of research on family functioning and delinquency is offered as a means of outlining the empirical knowledge that was used to build the current ecological investigation.

Conceptual Issues Regarding Family Functioning and Delinquency

Family theory has cultivated a rich field of literature that overlaps family therapy, and incorporates conceptual models of family interactions, and specific schemes for measurement of family processes. These measurement models propose complex constructions that verge on minor family theories. Conceptual models include the Distance Regulation Model (Kantor & Lehr, 1990), and the Paradigmatic Model (Constantine, 1986).

Several scales have also been developed to measure internal family functions and their relationship to clinical issues. These scales include the Family Environment Scale (Moos & Moos, 1981); the Beavers-Timberlawn Family Evaluation Scale (Beavers, 1985); the Family Assessment Device (Epstein & Bishop, 1983); and the Family Adaptability and Cohesion Evaluation Scales (Olson, Portner, & Bell, 1982). While each of these tools has relative strengths, the latter was chosen to measure family functioning variables in this study (see Chapter 5).

Linkages of family processes and delinquent behavior have been studied extensively. These studies usually emerge from the family systems or criminology perspectives. Two primary processes of family functioning that notably assert themselves in the family and delinquency literature are family cohesion and parental control. As is made evident through thoughtful reading of the literature, various theorists and researchers use only mildly variant terms to refer to remarkably similar constructs. Family cohesion, parental attachment, parental bonding, affectionate bonding, and family emotional support, may all be thought of as representing the connectedness or attachment between the adolescent and his or her parent(s) (Beavers, 1985; Epstein & Bishop, 1983; Olson, Portner, & Bell, 1982; Moos & Moos, 1981). Likewise, terms such as parental leadership, parental monitoring, discipline, family problem-solving, and family adaptability share a common theme which may be seen as the family process of parental control (Beavers, 1985; Epstein & Bishop, 1983; Olson, Portner, Bell, 1982; Moos & Moos, 1981).

Research on the Relationship of Family Cohesion and Parental Control to Delinquency

Several studies have been conducted to outline the relationship between various factors of family functioning and delinquent behavior. These studies have consistently focused on aspects of family cohesion and parental control. They are briefly reviewed below.

A paradigm shift in intervention with delinquents occurred when Structural Family Therapy was initially articulated (Minuchin, Montalvo, Guerney, Rosman, & Schumer, 1967). It emerged from a clinically oriented action-research effort at the Wiltwyck School for Boys, which was a residential center serving the delinquent population of New York City in the late 1960's. The influence of Structural Family Therapy has been both broad and deep in the clinical field (Nichols & Schwartz, 2001). Since its earliest applications to families of delinquents, it has been used in work with diverse populations and presenting problems.

This seminal research produced an outline of the structure of low-income families of male delinquents, many of whom were African-American and Latino. With a focus on family relationship patterns, the authors identified two extreme forms, which they termed "enmeshment" (dysfunctional emotional closeness between parent and child) and "disengagement" (dysfunctional emotional distance between parent and child). The investigators noted that, in their sample, fathers or stable father figures were absent. This family composition left child rearing completely to the mother. While the researchers were careful not to attribute extreme forms of functioning to single parent families in general, they noted that in the families studied, the mothers were available for attachment and nurture needs, but anxious about having to provide control functions. In enmeshed families, mothers would experience their sons' acting out as their own personal failure, which evoked a complimentary response in the son. The authors summarized this response as, "If I steal, I hurt my mother", rather than, "If I steal, I am a thief." They concluded that the child does not learn to take responsibility for his actions, because there is no clear demarcation between the behavior or self-perception of the mother and child. In disengaged families, the mother would rarely inquire about the day-to-day life of the child, thereby abdicating the supervision role required of parents. The authors concluded that neither of these extremes in family cohesion, enmeshment nor disengagement, prepares the child for dealing with stress and conflict, or for focusing attention on solutions to problems external to the family. They also identified the crucial role of parents using their power benevolently to install limits on child behavior. Implicit in this approach are the family functions of cohesion and control, which resurface in much of the research on delinquency. Also indicated, is the primary role of stress and coping factors in adolescent adjustment.

A study conducted by Towberman (1994), examined associations between selected psychosocial variables and chronic delinquency, conducted a factor analysis of the related variables, and regressed these factors onto chronic delinquency. Of all the derived factors, including a diverse array of variables that are relevant to the current study, such as placement history, offense history, age at adjudication, educational involvement, and prior victimization, only the family cohesion factor significantly predicted all the included dimensions of chronic delinquency. This sample included a small percentage of females, and was primarily African-American. The study, therefore, suggests that family cohesion may be related to repeated delinquent acts within the population of interest in this book.

In a study designed to uncover supports that mediate the impact of stressors on adolescents, it was found that emotional support from the family is a powerful mediator of peer stressors in the development of adolescent depression (Wenz-Gross, Siperstein, Untch, & Widaman, 1997). While depression is not a form of delinquency, many clinicians have noted a close connection of the two phenomena (Samuels & Sikorsky, 1990). Although the findings reported in this study do not directly apply to the relationship between family functioning and delinquent behavior, they do indicate that family functioning is involved in the youth's affective experience of stressors. As noted in the review of stress, coping, and delinquency, many investigators have convincingly linked these variables.

In an attempt to incorporate ethnicity in an examination of family processes and delinquency, Vazroni and Flannery (1997), found that higher levels of family cohesion were negatively correlated with delinquent behaviors. Their sample included European-Americans and African-Americans in early adolescence, and it was determined that family variables explained more variance for the European-Americans than for the African-Americans. They also found that parental monitoring was negatively correlated with delinquent behavior, meaning that higher levels of parental control were associated with lower levels of delinquent behavior. This study lends support to the proposition that both cohesion and control factors may have effect and significance in preventing the generation of delinquent behaviors. It also suggests that there may be a significant difference in the degree to which family factors affect the manifest delinquency of two racial groups.

Len (1988) interviewed 63 incarcerated adults regarding the connections they made between parental discipline and their own criminal behavior. While 70% were incarcerated for crimes against persons, and 81% reported suffering harsh parental punishment or violent abuse, only 12 of the 63 verbalized a connection between their experience of abuse and their subsequent violent offenses. The author points out that the criminal tradition of "doing your own time" may involve a form of rugged individualism which mitigates against openly admitting that anyone else had responsibility for the decision to commit crimes. While this may be plausible, it appears to be more likely that emphasis should be placed on the individual inmate's identity as a powerful person who has been able to affect others, rather than as a victim of parental maltreatment. The psychological construct of "identification with the aggressor" may be operative in such a circumstance. Another psychological explanation offered for this finding is the expectation that the child is supposed to love his or her parents even though the parents beat the child (Len, 1988). While the perception of inmates is certainly valuable in understanding the ways in which they may process their own life events, the high level of statistical association between parental disciplinary practices and their children's commission of violent crimes in this sample cannot be taken lightly.

In an investigation of the relationship between family processes and self-reported and official delinquency records, interviews and record reviews of all seventh and eighth graders in Rochester, N.Y. were completed (Krohn, Stern, Thornberry, & Jang, 1992). This study used a sample that was mostly male and African-American, but no gender or race comparisons were conducted. Correlations were calculated to display associations between several family cohesion and parental control variables with both self-reported and officially recorded delinquency. Both parents and their adolescent children were asked to provide data on the family processes. For both parents and adolescents, high ratings on cohesion variables such as "attachment" and "involvement" were negatively associated with both self-reported and official measures of delinquency. In addition, the control variable "supervision" demonstrated the same pattern. For the adults, "consistency of discipline" was negatively associated with both delinquency measures, while it was only associated with self-reported delinquency for the adolescents. For the adolescents, also negatively associated with self-reported delinquency were "positive parenting" and "communication". These may be perceived as factors which integrate aspects of cohesion and control. This study indicates that both family cohesion and parental control may operate as buffers against delinquent activity.

Sheilds and Clarke (1995) studied the relationships of family cohesion and parental control with self-reported delinquency. The authors noted that previous research indicated that positive affective family interactions, including acceptance and responsiveness to child needs are negatively associated with delinquent behaviors. A parental control strategy, which establishes flexible limits without being excessively demanding, has also been negatively associated with delinquency. In this investigation, the sample consisted of 480 adolescents, slightly over half of whom were male, with only 13% of "minority" status. For these young people, high "family cohesion" was negatively associated with delinquency. For reasons that are unclear, however, no significant relationships were found between the degree of flexibility in parental control and delinquency. This finding is not consistent with those of many similar studies, but it is supported by one that focused on the differential effects of these variables for two racial groups.

Gray-Ray and Ray (1990) reported that differences exist in the influence of family characteristics on delinquent behavior, when comparing African-American and European-American youth. While the often-established inverse relationships between parental control and family cohesion held for European-American youth, only the existence of parental rejection (an indicator of low family cohesion) showed a positive relationship to delinquency among African-American youth in this study. These uncommon results may be important in developing an understanding of the specific situation of African-American male delinquents, but it is necessary to note that other studies have yet to replicate these results.

In a study of 362 low income African-American and Latino youth, a subgroup of violent offenders reported poorer discipline, less cohesion, and less involvement in their families than did the non-offending or non-violent offending subgroups. The researchers were not able to differentiate the violent, non-offending, and non-violent offending subgroups by their history or frequency of delinquent behavior or age at onset of delinquent behavior (Gorman-Smith, Tolan, Zelli, & Huesmann, 1996). In addition, it was found that the African-American youth from families with stronger beliefs in family duty and family loyalty were less likely to be violent delinquents than those who came from families with weaker beliefs in these values. This study suggests that both cohesion and control may play a role in the generation of delinquent behavior among African-American youth.

As a body, studies of the associations of cohesion and control with delinquency provide firm support for the primary role of the relationship between parents and their children as a protection against the commission and maintenance of illegal adolescent acts. Consistent across investigations, is the significant and powerful effect of sustained parental efforts to value the child, be responsive to the child's needs, and maintain some developmentally appropriate connection into the child's adolescence.

In addition, the notable, but somewhat less substantiated contribution of parental control may operate in the form of a non-linear, or threshold, function where "too much" or "too little" relates to delinquent behavior, and "just enough" provides a protective factor. Also unclear is how important it is for the child to perceive parental functioning positively, and whether the parental control action works effectively even if the child resents it at the time. It also may be that parental discipline is really confounded with cohesion, in that only parents who care and are attached to their children will provide consistent yet flexible limits.

Since findings reveal that extreme forms of discipline are associated with delinquency, it is likely that harsh or violent parental actions are experienced as something other than cohesion by the youth, but the actual operation of this dynamic requires further amplification. These characteristics may be more reflective of limited parenting skills, parental self-absorption, or inaccurate parental assessment of the needs of the child. In other words, a parent who attempts to control child behaviors with harsh actions, may be responding with limited resources, or out of a desire to limit the child's behavior for the adult's own benefit.

Although current knowledge in this area provides a valuable foundation for effective action, it appears that further research on these issues is warranted. Particular associations among the factors of family cohesion, parental control, and delinquency for African-American youth should be investigated more specifically.

CHAPTER 5

Problem, Participants, and Procedures

This chapter includes sections that present a statement of the problem addressed in the current research, a description of the selection of participants, an explanation of the procedures used to collect and organize data, a presentation of the research design, discussion of the measures applied, and an outline of data analysis techniques employed.

STATEMENT OF THE PROBLEM

As may be gathered from the included review of the historical and research literature, a great deal of effort has been directed toward uncovering the connections between personal and environmental factors in the production of delinquent behaviors in adolescents. Taken together, prior research has been successful in developing separate pictures of successive levels of the social ecology. It is clear that social factors such as limited opportunity, personal experience of stress and coping, and family functioning in the areas of cohesion and control, are linked to delinquent behaviors. A reasonable case has also been made regarding the inequitable representation of African-American males in secure settings across the United States, and the mounting risk of increasingly punitive responses to juvenile crimes committed by this group of youth.

There are, however, some gaps in existing knowledge as it relates to these issues. The specific needs of African-American youth have not been systematically investigated. Prior research indicates that there are at least some relationships among relevant variables that differ for sub-samples of African-American and European-American youth, but no located studies focus comprehensively and exclusively on these issues as they pertain to the group of youth which is at greatest risk for out-of-home placement. Therefore, only limited knowledge is available regarding the social ecologies of these youth.

A linkage of delinquency and placement has been assumed in much of the literature, but when one focuses on out-of-home placement, such a linkage should not be taken for granted. Although at least one delinquent act is generally required for the first out-of-home placement to occur, subsequent placements may be independent of additional delinquency. Clarity regarding patterns of placement and specification of models of environmental and personal factors, which mediate or explain repeated confinements, have not been made available.

This study may be located as an extension of the literature on delinquency, with a specification of the associations of personal and environmental variables that perpetuate a high risk situation for a growing population of American youth. In this way, the present study attempts to address intellectual, moral, social, and practical problems. Intellectually, there is a challenge to specify ecological linkages of the person-in-environment and apply a methodology that extends the correlational approach to focus on the feedback in natural systems. Morally, the disproportionate rate of confinement for African-American youth requires better understanding and improved intervention. The social problem of delinquency and the expenditure of public resources for control and change of specified groups is one of historical proportions that still requires more effective bases for decision-making. Finally, on a practical level, the efforts of policy-makers and treatment providers may benefit from a clearer understanding and an expanded view of the needs and risks encountered by African-American male youth.

While this study provides some answers to the questions raised by a review of the existing literature, it is apparent that the use of an existing data set, the restrictions of a retrospective and correlational design, and the non-probability sample drawn, impose limitations on the external validity of its findings. In this way, the intended goal is incremental knowledge rather than grand theory building or sweeping systemic change. This goal is modest, but important. The purpose of this study is to contribute to understanding the problem of disproportionate confinement of African-American males in facilities that house delinquent youth. To do so, variables that represent levels of the youths' social ecologies are analyzed.

PARTICIPANT SAMPLE

Participants in this study were drawn from the total population of African-American male adolescents placed at a large Midwestern residential agency during the full operation of the agency's clinical information system from 1985 to 1993. They may be considered to comprise a purposive sample, as they were selected by the criteria of race, gender, official report of delinquency, out-of-home placement, and completion of a full set of clinical assessment instruments (described below in the Measures section). The completion of the clinical measures was the only known difference at the time of analysis, between these youth and the remainder of the African-American males placed at the agency during this period. Including the variables contained in the clinical measures was crucial to the ecological focus of this study. The total sample numbers 171. A more thorough presentation of selected participant characteristics is included in Chapter 6 as part of the descriptive analysis.

DATA MANAGEMENT PROCEDURES

This study took place in the context of an agency that serves delinquent youth in multiple locations. The host agency was selected for a number of reasons. It is a large private agency that serves delinquent youth and their families and provides a range of services to diverse clients. Its out-of-home placements cover the spectrum from community-based group homes to campus based residential settings and detention facilities.

Data for this study were collected through client intake procedures and clinically-relevant measures that were integrated into the clinical information system of the host agency (Grasso & Epstein, 1987). They may be considered to be archival data, in that they were routinely collected into an historical database.

Agency staff were responsible for data collection. Measures were obtained at the initiation of the most recent out-of-home placement (intake to an agency program), except for release data which were necessarily obtained at the termination of placement. Demographics and offense history were retrieved from case files, and through an interview by the intake worker. Stress, coping, and family functioning data were obtained through self-report from participants. Placement termination data were reported by a staff member of the youth's treatment team.

At each agency site, the intake worker was responsible for completion of the intake form following an interview of the youth, parent if available, and the delinquency services worker. The family therapist administered the clinical measures of stressors, coping strategies, and family functioning to the youth. The treatment director reported case closing information at the point of release from the placement. All staff who contributed to data collection were trained in data collection techniques, and provided with a research manual, which documented responsibilities and procedures as well as definitions of all terms.

The purposes of data collection (for assessment of individual treatment needs, and further study of aggregate characteristics of the agency's client population), were fully explained to participants by the intake worker, assent obtained from the youth, and informed consent obtained from a responsible adult guardian (parent and/or delinquency services worker). Participants verbally agreed to complete the clinical assessment instruments for treatment and research purposes. All participants indicated that they understood that they were not compelled to complete the instruments; they could choose which information, if any, to submit; that all treatment services would be provided regardless of completion of the instruments; and that any youth (or guardian) could choose to terminate participation in the study at any time, without penalty.

Each participant was issued a unique numeric identifier to ensure confidentiality and facilitate data tracking. No list of names or other means of identifying participants by name was available to the researcher, therefore, anonymity exists within the study.

The placement and ecological variables were entered into a specially constructed data file for this analysis. The distribution for each of these variables was analyzed and treated according to accepted statistical principles (Tabachnick & Fidell, 1996). Categorical variables were recoded as dichotomous variables for inclusion in the regression models.

RESEARCH DESIGN

This study employed a retrospective correlational design. Variables were measured for a single sample and subsequently analyzed. Measures of demographics, offense history, youth clinical characteristics, family characteristics, and placement history were taken at the time of the youth's intake into the program.

Demographic variables include age at intake, and urban/non-urban environment. Offense history variables include number of status offenses, number of felony offenses, and number of adjudications. Youth clinical characteristics include stressors in the form of family tensions, and coping as indicated by personal investment and ventilation. Family characteristics include family composition, and family functioning. Placement history includes living situation at time of intake and number of prior placements.

Program completion and aftercare variables were measured at the youth's release from the program. Program completion variables include an assessment of successful completion of treatment goals, length of stay, and type of release. The aftercare variable captures the type of post-release placement.

The psychometric properties of the clinical assessment instruments were tested and the measures were improved for this sample. Descriptive information about the sample was summarized, the representativeness of the sample for the agency population was assessed, and bivariate associations among the intake and completion variables were computed, as were their respective associations with total out-of-home placements, for each case. Preliminary work for path analysis was completed. Aggregate data were used in Multiple Regression Analyses to identify the relative contributions of selected blocks of variables to an explanation of out-of-home placements for youth in the sample. Each block of variables represents a specific category of ecological variables including demographics, offense history, youth clinical characteristics, and family characteristics. An additional block that combines features from each level of the youth's social ecology was also tested to assess its relative value for explanation of out-of-home placements.

The research design is represented in Figure 2, which shows the measures used at each data collection point and the analysis conducted. Although such a design suffers from inherent limits on the control of variables and threats to external validity, it retains notable utility in this application. The design used in this study carries the advantages of access to a reasonably sized and homogeneous sample of confined African-American males. It possesses the potential for in-depth quantitative examination of the relationships among several relevant variables at the personal, family, and community levels. It provides greater opportunity to develop understanding about this sample than would be possible in a controlled experiment, based on the limited state of knowledge about this problem.

It is true that the use of an existing dataset carries the convenience of readily accessible data, but this advantage is often compromised by the need to extensively clean the data and reject any cases for which information is suspect. This form of data collection was, therefore, chosen for more than its mere convenience. It is important to note that the comprehensiveness of these data are necessary to inform an ecological investigation. A non-experimental design also obviates moral difficulties with random selection and assignment of minority youth to confined conditions and attendant compromises to public safety. The strengths and limitations of this design are further discussed in Chapter 7.

MEASURES

In addition to agency-developed forms, measures used in this study included standardized assessment inventories designed for research and practice. These were selected by the agency to provide information that would be useful for intervention and investigation such as the present study. They are outlined in Figure 3, and described in detail below.

Intake Form

The Intake Form is an agency-developed tool that was designed to collect client characteristics at entry. A single trained staff member at each agency site completed the form to ensure consistency in data

Figure 2: Research Design

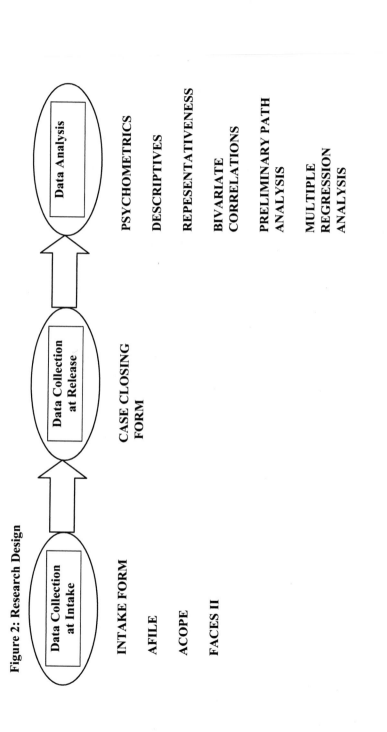

collection. Variables were measured primarily at the nominal level, except where ordinal level counts could be assigned.

Variables from the Intake Form that are used in the analyses include, Age at Intake, County of Residence (Urban Environment), Status Offenses, Felony Offenses, and Adjudications, Family Type (Single Parent Family), Intake Living Situation (Intake from Home), and Prior Placements.

Adolescent-Family Inventory of Life Events and Changes (A-FILE)

Growing out of research and practice with family stress across the life cycle, the A-FILE is a fifty item self-report instrument designed to record normative and non-normative life events and changes an adolescent perceives his or her family has experienced during the past twelve months (McCubbin, Patterson, Bauman & Harris, 1981). A-FILE also records these events as experienced prior to the past year. The instrument provides an index of the adolescent's vulnerability to the stressors encountered by all family members. A-FILE was developed for completion by adolescents of junior and senior high school age (from 12-18 years of age). As a family life-change inventory, all events experienced by any family member are recorded. Each item in the A-FILE was worded, according to the authors, to reflect a change of sufficient magnitude to require some adjustment in the regular pattern or behavior of family members (McCubbin, Thompson, McCubbin, 1996).

The primary measure derived from A-FILE is Total Family Life Changes. Internal reliability (Chronbach's Alpha) for the overall scale is .69. Reliability was assessed with a sample of 74 junior and senior high school students in their homes, and again two weeks later in their schools. No other information is available about this sample. Observed test-retest reliability is .82 at a two-week interval.

Validity of the original instrument was addressed by its developers through use of data from a sample of 500 junior and senior high school youth. Three procedures were used to reduce the item pool to the final 50 items. They include, an analysis of the frequencies of occurrence of all the items, factor analysis followed by tests of internal reliability and test-retest reliability, and reference to prior research and theories regarding family life changes (McCubbin, Thompson, McCubbin, 1996).

Figure 3: Measures and Variables at Time of Data Collection

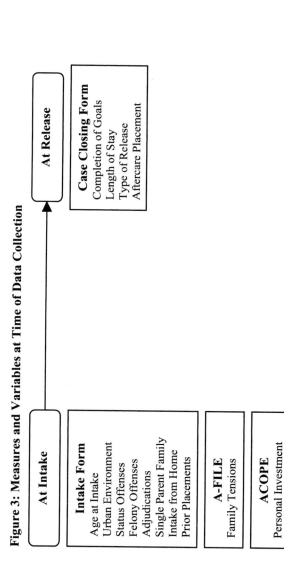

At Intake

Intake Form
Age at Intake
Urban Environment
Status Offenses
Felony Offenses
Adjudications
Single Parent Family
Intake from Home
Prior Placements

A-FILE
Family Tensions

ACOPE
Personal Investment
Ventilation

FACES II
Family Functioning

At Release

Case Closing Form
Completion of Goals
Length of Stay
Type of Release
Aftercare Placement

Subscales, with their respective internal and test-retest reliabilities, include Family Transitions (.53/.80), Sexuality (.45/.90), Losses (.46/.82), Responsibilities and Strains (.76/.69), Substance Use (.63/.81), and Legal Conflict.(.62/.81).

A review of the literature on development of the A-FILE indicated that the subscales were not constructed through exploratory factor analysis, but rather by conceptually clustering items into types or categories of stressors (McCubbin & Patterson 1991). A subsequent factor analytic procedure was used to assign factor loadings to the items and compute the scale reliabilities. Such an approach is based on recognition that the items refer to events, and that contact with a particular stressor will not necessarily correlate with that of another stressor, especially over the short time span to which these items are referenced. For example, two notable losses, such as the death of a parent and the death of a sibling, may not be statistically associated over the course of one year, unless there is a common cause of death such as the same accident, or a rapidly rising genetic predisposition. It is, perhaps, as likely that the death of a parent will not be related to the death of a sibling even though they may both be experienced and conceptually grouped as losses. From a logical perspective, therefore, exploratory factor analysis would not be an appropriate procedure to use to cluster items.

Attention has been paid to development of norms for a general population of youth in residential care and, specifically, for African-American youth in residential care (McCubbin, Thompson, McCubbin, 1996). For a general sample of 954 youth, the mean number of family life events and changes recorded by the A-FILE was 15.562 (SD 6.512). For a subsample of 446 African-American youth, the mean score was relatively unchanged, at 15.621 (SD 6.676). There are, however, no known attempts to reassess the psychometrics of the scales within the instrument for a homogeneous African-American sample.

Therefore, despite the careful approach taken by the developers of this instrument, it was deemed worthwhile to assess the properties of the derived scales using this African-American sample. In order to do so, a confirmatory factor analysis of the A-FILE scales was conducted. The reader is referred to Chapter 6 for extensive description of this analysis and the processing of its results.

This analysis indicated that the original subscales of the A-FILE, even when modified by careful elimination of poorly performing items, would not pass statistical tests that are commonly used to confirm appropriate measurement characteristics. Subscales of the A-FILE did not show enough difference from one another to warrant their inclusion in the analyses for this study. Even when all the items from the A-FILE were tested as a single stress scale, this scale did not show strong enough distinctiveness from other clinical characteristics such as coping strategies and family functioning to be used in the current analysis.

In order to incorporate a valid measure of stressors in this ecological investigation, it was necessary to thoroughly reorganize the A-FILE items. A new scale, named Family Tensions, was constructed through application of a conceptual strategy similar to that used by the original authors of the instrument, and validated through confirmatory factor analysis (see Chapter 6). Items that address arguments and conflicts within the family were selected, and tested in a confirmatory factor analysis with the items of the original subscales of Losses and Transitions. The Family Tensions scale passed tests for distinctiveness from other factors, and internal fit of the items. It achieved an alpha coefficient of .71, which demonstrates acceptable internal consistency.

Family Tensions was included as the only stressor measure in the correlation and regression analyses. Its inclusion is consistent with theory and clinical knowledge about the sample. Original A-FILE items assigned to Family Tensions and their new factor loadings are shown in Table 1. Review of this table will help the reader form a clear idea of the type of stressors that the youth in this sample perceived their families to experience, and to understand the relative importance of each item as a part of the scale. Items capture changes related to emotional problems; parental arguments; and arguments between parents and teenagers related to use of the car or hours away from home, friends and social activities, religious activities, personal appearance, and completion of household chores. An additional item addresses pressure to perform well in academics or athletics.

**Table 1: Family Tensions Items from A-FILE with New Factor
         Loadings**

A-FILE ITEM #	A-FILE ITEM	FACTOR LOADING
29.	A family member has emotional problems.	.41
37.	Increase in arguments between parents.	.60
39.	Parents and teenagers have increased arguments over use of the car or hours to stay out.	.57
40.	Parents and teenagers have increased arguments over choice of friends and/ or social activities.	.48
41.	Parents and teenagers have increased arguments over attendance at religious activities.	.57
42.	Parents and teenagers have increased arguments over personal appearance (clothes, hair, etc.)	.39
43.	Increased arguments over getting jobs done at home.	.52
44.	Increased pressure for a member in school to get "good" grades or do well in sports or school activities.	.32

Adolescent Coping Orientation for Problem Experiences (ACOPE)

ACOPE is a 54 item self-report instrument that was designed to
identify the behaviors adolescents find helpful in managing problems or
difficult situations as they strive for a functional balance of
independence and connection with parents (Patterson & McCubbin,
1983). In concert with developmental theory, the instrument provides
information about the coping strategies the adolescent prefers to use
when faced with personal or family stressors, or difficult life changes in
general. The instrument was informed by the developmental task of
identity formation, and accepts the assumption that during the critical

transitional period from childhood to adolescence, the young person will struggle with staying connected to and dependent on the family, while trying to exercise his or her need for increasing independence (McCubbin, Thompson, McCubbin, 1996).

Development of the ACOPE instrument progressed from structured interviews with a total of 30 males and females who were enrolled in the 10th, 11th, and 12th grades. These interviews yielded responses describing what the youth did to manage the hardships and relieve the discomfort for the most difficult stressor they experienced, the most difficult stressor experienced by their families, and for difficult life changes in general. Ninety-five items resulted. These were reduced by analyzing the responses of a different group of 467 adolescents, and eliminating items that were "never used", as well as those that did not survive factor analytic techniques (McCubbin, Thompson, McCubbin, 1996). No other information is available about these adolescent samples.

The resulting 54 items were shaped into 12 subscales that are labeled as coping strategies. These subscales and their internal consistency reliabilities include Ventilation (.75), Low Level Activity (.75), Self-Reliance (.69), Emotional Connections (.75), Family Problem-Solving (.71), Passive Problem-Solving (.71), Spiritual Support (.72), Friendship Support (.76), Professional Support (.50), High Activity Level (.67), Humor (.72), and Relaxation (.60).

Several prior analyses have been conducted to illuminate the use of these coping strategies by various groups of youth with different characteristics. One, of particular interest to the present examination, compared the relative use of these coping strategies by African-American and "Caucasian" youth of single parent families (McCubbin, Thompson, McCubbin, 1996). Differences were not tested for statistical significance, but visual analysis indicates that there may be relevant differences in the use of Ventilation (African-American mean 14.71/ SD 4.32; Caucasian mean 17.19/ SD 4.80), Passive Problem Solving (African-American mean 10.98/ SD 3.91; Caucasian mean 15.10/ SD 4.77), and Spiritual Support (African-American mean 8.04/ SD 3.16; Caucasian mean 5.90/ SD 2.71).

The primary developers of the ACOPE recognized that greater sensitivity to the particular coping strategies of African-American youth in residential care might be valuable to practitioners, so they revised the original scales with such a sample (McCubbin, Thompson, Elver, 1996). Their intent was to increase ethnic sensitivity, yet maintain an instrument that would be applicable to Caucasian as well as African-American youth. The resultant instrument was named the Youth Coping Index (YCI). The 31 items used in the YCI were drawn from the 54 items of the ACOPE. Through analysis of scores recorded by 91 African-American youth in residential placement, three subscales were derived. Overall youth coping has an internal reliability of .86, while the subscales of "Incendiary Communication and Tension Mangement", "Spiritual and Personal Development", and "Positive Appraisal and Problem Solving" were shown to have internal reliabilities of .70, .84, and .79, respectively.

Short-term test-retest reliability coefficients were not made available. The reported test-retest reliability for this instrument over 6 to 15 months is .43. Long-term reliability for "Spiritual and Personal Development" is .44, "Youth Positive Appraisal and Problem Solving" is .33, and Incendiary Communication and Tension Management" is .19. These values are notably quite low. It is possible, however, that they were confounded by the effects of an intervening treatment program over the 6-15 month span.

The only reported validity check on the YCI was published by the developers in the context of a study that attempted to predict program completion and post-release living situation at 3 and 12 months for a group of youth released from residential care for juvenile delinquency (McCubbin, Fleming, Thompson, Neitman, Elver, & Savas, 1995). For the African-American subsample in this study, the "Incendiary Communication and Tension Management" subscale significantly predicted program completion and successful adaptation at 3 and 12 months. Neither "Spiritual and Personal Development" nor "Positive Appraisal and Problem Solving", however, showed any significant relationship to the selected outcomes. One must conclude that only limited validity has been demonstrated for the YCI.

The YCI was also unavailable at the time of data collection for this study. Therefore, confirmatory factor analysis was conducted to assess the psychometric properties of the ACOPE instrument for this sample of African-American male delinquents. For more information about this analysis and its results, please see Chapter 6. Despite exhaustive attempts to maintain versions of the original ACOPE subscales, most did not meet acceptable levels of internal consistency and distinctiveness from one another for this sample.

Two factors emerged from this confirmatory factor analysis. The original Ventilation scale was supported. Its internal consistency coefficient (alpha) for this sample was .72. A new scale was derived and named Personal Investment, because it encompassed applications of various personal strengths to developing and caring for one's self. Personal Investment showed an internal reliability of .80. In addition, both of these factors passed tests for internal consistency and distinctiveness when included in a factor analysis with the stressor and family functioning items from the A-FILE and the FACES II (see Chapter 6).

Original ACOPE items and their factor loadings in the newly derived Ventilation scale are shown in Table 2. They include items related to getting angry and yelling at people, complaining to family members, swearing, blaming others, and saying mean sarcastic things to people. Also indicated in Table 2, by items with an asterisk, is the fact that all five of these items were also included in the "Incendiary Communication and Tension Management" subscale of the YCI. The YCI subscale, however, also includes three additional items, so there are notable differences between the results that produced the YCI and those of the present factor analysis. The new Ventilation scale also has

**Table 2: Ventilation Items from ACOPE with New Factor
      Loadings**

ACOPE ITEM #	ACOPE ITEM	FACTOR LOADING
19.	Get angry and yell at people. *	.74
22.	Let off steam by complaining to family members. *	.40
26.	Swear. *	.45
28.	Blame others for what's going on. *	.78
49.	Say mean things to people; be sarcastic. *	.57

* these items are also included in the YCI scale "Incendiary Communication and Tension Management".

Disproportionate Confinement

the advantage of parsimony when compared to the ACOPE and the YCI because it is composed of fewer items.

Items from the ACOPE that comprise Personal Investment are shown in Table 3. They include actions such as getting more involved in school activities, improving self by getting good grades or exercising, organizing one's life, working hard on projects, helping others solve their problems, doing things with the family, and sleeping.

Also indicated in Table 3, by items with an asterisk, is the fact that six of these seven items are also included in either the 13-item "Spiritual and Personal Development" subscale, or the 10-item "Positive Appraisal and Problem Solving" subscale of the YCI. One item, related to sleeping, is not included in either of the YCI subscales. The new Personal Investment scale has the advantage of parsimony when compared to the ACOPE and the YCI because it is composed of fewer items.

Table 3: Personal Investment Items from ACOPE with New Factor Loadings

ACOPE ITEM #	ACOPE ITEM	FACTOR LOADING
10.	Get more involved in activities at school. *	.67
13.	Try to improve yourself (get body in shape, get better grades, etc.) *	.64
25.	Organize your life and what you have to do. *	.66
27.	Work hard on schoolwork or other projects. *	.73
30.	Try to help other people solve theirproblems. *	.61
41.	Do things with your family. *	.63
48.	Sleep.	.46

* these items are also included in the YCI scales "Spiritual and Personal Development" or "Positive Appraisal and Problem Solving".

Family Adaptability and Cohesion Evaluation Scales (FACES II)

Based on family theory and family therapy, the FACES II is a 30 item self-report measure that is designed to identify the degree of adaptability and cohesion employed by a family (Olson, Portner & Bell, 1982). Family Adaptability is defined as the ability of the family system to change its power structure, role relationships, and relationship rules in response to situational and developmental stress. It is a concept that captures the degree of flexibility that the family uses to change in the face of life demands. Family Cohesion is defined as the emotional bonding family members experience with one-another. Communication is also measured by the instrument, but is considered to be a "facilitating" dimension that allows adaptability and cohesion to be manifested.

The initial FACES instrument was developed in doctoral dissertation research. It used 111 items, and established the primary dimensions of adaptability, cohesion, and communication (Olson, McCubbin, Barnes, Larsen, Muxen, & Wilson, 1982).

The FACES II was developed to reduce the number of items to 30, improve readability, and improve psychometric properties (Olson, McCubbin, Barnes, Larsen, Muxen, & Wilson, 1982). Fifty items were tested on 464 adults with an average age of 30.5. No other information about this sample is provided, but a further national sample of 2,412 individuals was used to reduce the items to 30 from 50. This sample has been described as "predominantly Lutheran and white" (Fredman & Sherman, 1987). Subsequent research challenged the orthogonality (or independence) of the two primary dimensions by demonstrating that they were highly intercorrelated.

Developers of the instrument made a third attempt to utilize similar scales, which they named FACES III (Olson, Portner, & Lavee, 1985). FACES III became a 20 item instrument which demonstrated considerable improvement in independence of the adaptability and cohesion scales (Fredman & Sherman, 1987). Nonetheless, the FACES II demonstrated better reliability of the adaptability scale (Fredman & Sherman, 1987). For this reason, and reasons of familiarity, it maintained greater popularity than the FACES III with many clinicians.

A further iteration of this measurement has been offered in the form of the Family Attachment and Changeability Index 8 (McCubbin, Thompson, & Elver, 1995). The Family Attachment and Changeability

Index 8 (FACI 8) is a 16 item instrument that attempted to address the problems of the FACES instruments with curvilinearity, intercorrelations between the two primary scales, and the paucity of data confirming their applicability to families of color. The authors state that the FACI 8 was specifically developed to study African-Americans in residential placement. The FACI 8 renames the Cohesion dimension of the FACES as "Attachment". It also renames the Adaptability dimension as "Changeability".

The Attachment scale uses 8 items of the FACES II, and demonstrates an internal consistency coefficient (alpha) of .73. The Changeability scale also uses 8 items from the FACES II, and achieved an internal consistency coefficient of .80. No information has been made available about the distinctiveness of the scales from one another.

On its face, this would appear to be a highly relevant instrument for measurement of the variables in this study. It was not available at the time of data collection, however, and it has also not yet been shown to demonstrate acceptable construct validity (McCubbin, Thompson, McCubbin, 1996).

The FACES II was the most well-developed measure of these dimensions at the time of data collection. As measured by the FACES II instrument, the dimension of Adaptability has an internal reliability of .78, and includes the sub-dimensions of Assertiveness, Leadership (Control), Discipline, Negotiation, Roles, and Rules. These sub-dimensions closely approximate the aspects of Parental Control that were noted in the literature review reported in Chapter 4.

The dimension of Cohesion has a computed reliability of .87 and includes the sub-dimensions of Emotional Bonding, Family Boundaries, Coalitions, Time, Space, Friends, Decision-Making, and Interests and Recreation. These sub-dimensions capture the aspects of Family Cohesion that arose in the literature review.

Although the original conceptualization of these dimensions incorporated a complicated "Circumplex Model" wherein the dimensions were considered to be curvilinear, methodological and theoretical challenges have been mounted, and a linear interpretation is now considered to be more acceptable (Perosa & Perosa, 1990; Green, 1991; Olson & Tiesel, 1991). This means that it would be possible to type families according to their particular combination of the levels of Adaptability and Cohesion. Levels of Adaptability (from low to high) include Rigid, Structured, Flexible, and Chaotic. Levels of Cohesion (from low to high) include Disengaged, Separated, Connected, and Enmeshed.

By arranging the levels of Adaptability and Cohesion in a four-by-four figure, it is possible to identify sixteen distinct types of family functioning. These are shown in Figure 4. They include Chaotic-Disengaged, Chaotic-Separated, Chaotic-Connected, Chaotic-Enmeshed, Flexible-Disengaged, Flexible-Separated, Flexible-Connected, Flexible-Enmeshed, Structured-Disengaged, Structured-Separated, Structured-Connected, Structured-Enmeshed, Rigid-Disengaged, Rigid-Separated, Rigid-Connected, and Rigid-Enmeshed.

Respondents are asked to complete the instrument twice, once to provide their assessment of how things are now (Real), and then how they would like things to be (Ideal), so a measure of satisfaction is also possible. For purposes of this study, only the "Real" measure was considered.

A confirmatory factor analysis was conducted to assess the psychometric properties of the FACES II for this sample of African-American families of delinquents based on the youth's perception of the "Real" situation at the time. For further information about the result of this procedure, refer to Chapter 6. The original intent in this study was to use separate Parental Control and Family Cohesion factors, and a representation of family type (all based on the FACES model) in the correlation and regression analyses. Despite exhaustive attempts to maintain the original subscales of Adaptability and Cohesion, they did not show adequate psychometric properties as evidenced by combinations of strength and significance of internal consistency, and distinctiveness. In fact, the primary scales of Adaptability and Cohesion did not survive the confirmatory factor analysis and had to be discarded.

It was determined that for this sample, the distinction between Adaptability and Cohesion was not significantly measured by the FACES II instrument. Other researchers have also noted that there is an unacceptable intercorrelation between these two primary dimensions (McCubbin, Thompson, McCubbin, 1996). For these reasons, a single scale of Family Functioning was constructed. This scale consists of items that represent aspects of Family Cohesion and Parental Control. It produced an internal consistency coefficient (alpha) of .88. In

Figure 4: Sixteen Types of Family Functioning from FACES II

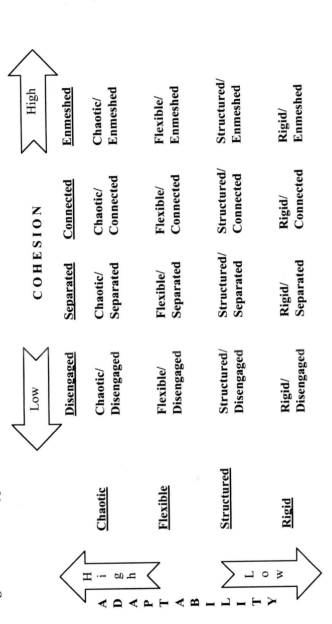

		COHESION		
	Low ⇦⇨ High			
	Disengaged	**Separated**	**Connected**	**Enmeshed**
Chaotic	Chaotic/ Disengaged	Chaotic/ Separated	Chaotic/ Connected	Chaotic/ Enmeshed
Flexible	Flexible/ Disengaged	Flexible/ Separated	Flexible/ Connected	Flexible/ Enmeshed
Structured	Structured/ Disengaged	Structured/ Separated	Structured/ Connected	Structured/ Enmeshed
Rigid	Rigid/ Disengaged	Rigid/ Separated	Rigid/ Connected	Rigid/ Enmeshed

ADAPTABILITY ⇧ High ⇩ Low

addition, it passed tests for distinctiveness when included in a factor analysis with the stressor and coping items from the A-FILE and the ACOPE. The Family Functioning scale is the best measure of cohesion and control that is allowed by the existing dataset, but it necessarily combines these two key factors of interest. A decision was made to enter the Family Functioning factor into the analyses, rather than to proceed with separate factors that were not adequately measured.

Original FACES II items that were retained in the Family Functioning factor are shown in Table 4 and Table 5. Table 4 shows items that were included in the original FACES II Cohesion scale. The items shown in Table 4 with asterisks are also included in the FACI 8 Attachment scale. Table 5 shows items that were included in the original FACES II Adaptability scale. The items shown in Table 5 with asterisks are also included in the FACI 8 Changeability scale.

It should be noted that only eight of the 14 surviving items are consistent with the 16 items of the FACI 8. Further, the analysis that produced the FACI 8 identified the two dimensions of Attachment

Table 4: Family Functioning Items from FACES II (Family Cohesion Scale) and New Factor Loadings

FACES II ITEM #	FACES II ITEM	FACTOR LOADING
1.	Family members are supportive of one another during difficult times.	.62
3.	It is easier to discuss problems with people outside the family than with other family members. *	.59
7.	Our family does things together.	.61
19.	Family members feel closer to people outside the family than to other family members. *	.63
21.	Family members go along with what the family decides to do.	.68

* these items are also included in the FACI 8 scale "Attachment".

(similar to the FACES II Cohesion dimension) and Changeability (like the FACES II Adaptability dimension), whereas the current factor analysis did not support the independence of these dimensions. This result may indicate that the FACES based instruments require further refinement in order to do an adequate job of measuring adaptability and cohesion for African-American male delinquents.

Table 5: Family Functioning Items from FACES II (Family Adaptability scale) and New Factor Loadings

FACES II ITEM #	FACES II ITEM	FACTOR LOADING
2.	In our family, it is easy for everyone to express his/her opinion. *	.61
4.	Each family member has input in major family decisions. *	.58
8.	Family members discuss problems and feel good about the solutions. *	.57
10.	We shift household responsibilities from person to person.	.52
16.	In solving problems, the children's suggestions are followed.	.57
18.	Discipline is fair in our family. *	.54
22.	In our family, everyone shares responsibilities. *	.67
26.	When problems arise, we compromise. *	.48

* these items are also included in the FACI 8 scale "Changeability".

Case Closing Report
The Case Closing Report is an agency-developed tool that was designed to record administrative and program completion information at the time the youth was released from the facility. Specific instructions for completion of all items were provided to staff members who routinely completed this form. Variables were measured primarily at the nominal and ordinal levels.

Variables included in the analyses for which data were collected on the Case Closing Report include Post Placement Destination (used in the computation of Total Out-of-Home Placements, and to determine Aftercare Placement Home), Length of Stay, and Reason for Release.

VARIABLES AND OPERATIONAL DEFINITIONS

It was not deemed practical to conduct an exhaustive investigation of all potentially relevant variables in this study. It must, therefore, be noted, that although racism is unmeasured in this study, it is assumed to be an environmental feature for this African-American sample. It may be embedded in urban environments that are essentially segregated, opportunities that are systematically limited, and juvenile justice system decisions that lead to placement. Other relevant factors such as variation in quality of legal advice and policies of individual judges have not been measured. Included variables, their definitions, and the instruments with which the data are gathered are listed below.

Dependent/Criterion Variables

This study was undertaken with a primary interest in confinements of African-American youth. Confinements are represented as out-of-home placements in detention facilities, community-based group homes, and residential facilities for delinquency intervention. Two forms of these out-of-home placements were measured in this study, including the number of placements and length of stay in the most recent agency placement.

The number of out-of-home placements was used in one of three forms, depending on the particular analysis conducted. The decision regarding which form to use was based on the logic required to make sure that only one form was used in each analysis, and to preserve the correct temporal order of variables. These three forms include *Prior Placements, Number of Placements, and Total Placements.*

Prior Placements is the number of out-of-home placements previous to the most recent agency placement, as recorded on the Intake Data Sheet. It was used in the correlational and multiple regression analyses, and as the basis for computation of the other placement variables.

Number of Placements is defined as the number of prior out-of-home placements, plus one for the most recent placement. It was used in the correlational and regression analyses.

Total Placements is a version of this variable that is computed by summing the number of prior placements, the most recent agency placement, and an out-of-home placement in the post-release period if one was implemented. *Total Placements* is used for the correlational schematic that takes into account all program variables.

Length of Stay (LOS) is a measure of the duration of the most recent confinement as recorded on the Case Closing Report. It is indicated by dates of intake and release, which are then used to compute units in months reported to two decimal places.

Independent/Predictor Variables

The following independent variables were selected to represent various levels of the participants' social ecologies. They are used to provide information about the experience of the youth that relates to out-of-home placement.

Age at Intake is recorded on the Intake Data Form. For purposes of this study, it is used in a computed form of years to two decimal places.

Family Type is recorded on the Intake Data Form. This categorical variable is recoded as the dichotomous variable *Single Parent Family* using dummy coding to represent Single Parent Family or Not Single Parent Family.

County of Residence is reported on the Intake Data Form. This categorical variable is recoded as the dichotomous variable *Urban Environment* in order to measure the contribution of an urban environment.

Intake Living Situation, which is the approved legal residence immediately prior to the most recent placement, was recorded on the Intake Data Form. This categorical variable was recoded as the dichotomous variable *Intake form Home.*

Status Offenses is defined as the number of status offenses officially reported in the case file and recorded on the Intake Data Form. Status offenses involve behaviors such as truancy, curfew violation, possession of tobacco, and incorrigibility that are violations of the law only when one has not yet reached the age of majority.

Felony Offenses is defined as the number of felony offenses officially reported in the case file and recorded on the Intake Data Form. Felony offenses are serious crimes against persons or property.

Adjudications is defined as the number of juvenile court adjudications officially reported in the case file and recorded on the Intake Data Form. Adjudications refer to juvenile court appearances wherein the adolescent was found guilty of a law violation.

The youth's contact with stressors is represented by the *Family Tensions* scale explained above. It was constructed from the included A-FILE items and was scored as a simple count of the youth's affirmative responses to the items, using the most recent 12 month time frame.

The youth's use of coping strategies is represented by the *Personal Investment* and *Ventilation* scales explained above. These were constructed from the ACOPE. Scale scores were calculated by obtaining the mean of all included item responses for each participant.

Parental Control and Family Cohesion are represented by the *Family Functioning* scale explained above. It was constructed from the FACES II. This scale was scored by obtaining the mean of all included item responses for each participant. Responses for reverse stated items were reverse scored (reflected) as outlined for the original instrument.

Successful program completion is measured by attainment of the agency's Integrated Treatment Plan Objectives as reported on the Case Closing Report. This is a staff assessment of the youth's progress toward the treatment goals that were outlined during the initial treatment planning conference. This categorical variable is recoded as the dichotomous variable *Successful Program Completion.*

Reason for Release is recorded on the Case Closing Report. Successful completion is defined by types of "acceptable" discharge from placement which includes a release that indicates the approval of the agency. This categorical variable was recoded as the dichotomous variable *Successful Release.*

Post Placement Destination is recorded on the Case Closing Report. This categorical variable is recoded as the dichotomous variable *Aftercare Home Placement.* This variable indicates that the youth's legal placement at the time of release was his family home or a "family-like" setting, such as regular foster care.

PLANNED ANALYSES
Multiple analyses were planned for the conduct of this study. They are outlined briefly below and their respective findings are presented in Chapter 6.

Psychometrics of Clinical Assessment Instruments
The measurement characteristics of the published clinical assessment instruments (A-FILE, ACOPE, and FACES II) were assessed using confirmatory factor analysis. Hunter's CFA program in Package was used for this analysis (Hunter & Hamilton, 1992). This was undertaken to establish the validity of these measures for an exclusively African-American male delinquent sample.

Initially, a separate confirmatory factor analysis of each instrument was run to test the overall measurement models and to identify and eliminate low quality items. Items that cross-loaded on two or more factors were eliminated, as were those whose factor loadings were less than .2. Next, a confirmatory factor analysis of all the surviving items from all three measures was run to test the independence of the stressor, coping, and family functioning constructs. These constructs were supported. This set of items was then used to fine tune new scales as described above, reviewed for conceptual clarity and then tested for item quality and independence of factors. The results of these factor tests are explicated in Chapter 6.

Description of Sample
Frequencies and distributions of all included variables were obtained to describe the characteristics of the participants. Mean and modal values were also used to construct a narrative description of the typical youth in this sample. The representativeness of the sample for the agency population of African-American males was assessed by comparing the two groups on several relevant variables.

Associations
Bivariate correlations among all pairs of included variables were obtained to identify significant relationships in the form of Pearson product-moment correlations, significant at the $p < .05$ level.

Schematics of Correlations

Correlational diagrams are used to present models of the observed variables that explain a youth's Total Out-of-Home Placements. Despite their appearance, it should be noted that these are not intended to represent causal models as constructed in path analysis. These diagrams were constructed *post-hoc*, using the observed correlations among the variables. The diagrams account for the temporal ordering of the variables and show the direction of their effects, but do not satisfy strict requirements regarding the *a-priori* ordering of variables that apply to structural equation modeling or other path modeling techniques. The schematics are presented in Chapter 6 for their heuristic value.

Multiple Regression Analysis

Standard multiple regression was used to explain two forms of out-of-home placement. Blocks of variables were regressed onto Number of Placements and Length of Stay, using a simultaneous procedure. The form of analysis used here may be interpreted as a way of comparing limited sets of independent variables to see which set best explains the dependent variables. The blocks were constructed on the bases of logical consistency of variables with others in the block, theoretical and practice value of understanding the contribution of the block, and temporal order of the variables.

CHAPTER 6

Relationships among Variables

This chapter presents the findings of the study. It provides the reader with the facts that were obtained from the research conducted, explanatory comments, and the author's description of what is important and noteworthy. Discussion of interpretations, implications, and meanings of the findings are presented.

Sections of this chapter include information about the confirmatory factor analyses, description of the sample, findings from the correlational analysis, findings from the regression analyses, and a presentation of the correlational schematic. These sections are structured to present results that are relevant to each respective research question and hypothesis.

RESEARCH QUESTIONS
The research questions emerged from practice and an interest in improving compliance with the policy mandate, as set forth in the juvenile justice code, to reduce disproportionate confinement of African-American male youth. They were specified through a review of the literature on disproportionate minority confinement and ecological factors that impact African-American delinquents. The research questions addressed, and their respective hypotheses are presented below.

Research Question 1: *What personal, family, and environmental characteristics describe African-American male delinquents who experience out-of-home placements?*

Hypothesis 1: The typical African-American male placed out of the home will be approximately sixteen years old, from a single-parent family, living in an urban environment, and will have been adjudicated for more   than one delinquent offense.

Hypothesis 2: This sample will not significantly differ from the agency population in age, offense history, or placement history.

Research Question 1 is directed toward illuminating important elements of the social ecology of African-American delinquents who experience confinement. This question is fundamental to the study in that it seeks a basic description of the ecological variables that exist in the lives of the youth in the sample. Descriptive statistics are used to address this question.

Hypothesis 1 uses a compound statement to outline the expected characteristics of the typical youth in the sample. These characteristics match those drawn from the literature as outlined in Chapter 4. The decision to group these characteristics, rather than state them each separately, matches the logic of describing the typical youth. This hypothesis, therefore, requires that all of the characteristics, as a set, describe the typical youth.

Hypothesis 2 states the expectation that the sample is representative of the agency population in terms of important demographic, offense, and placement variables. Confidence in the study's conclusions may be somewhat enhanced by demonstrated similarity of the sample to the agency population in these key areas.

Research Question 2: *What are the observed associations of personal, family, and environmental variables for African-American male delinquents who experience out-of-home placements?*

Hypothesis 3: Number of Placements will be significantly and positively correlated with Age at Intake, Status Offenses, Felony Offenses, Adjudications, Family Tensions, and use of the Ventilation coping strategy.

Hypothesis 4: Number of Placements will be significantly and negatively correlated with use of the Personal Investment coping strategy and Family Functioning.

Research Question 2 is directed toward uncovering the associations among the included variables as a way of identifying their relationships to each other. Bivariate correlations are obtained and tested in order to determine the strength and significance of these relationships.

Hypothesis 3 and Hypothesis 4 place special emphasis on the observed relationships of personal, family, and environmental variables with out-of-home placements. For each respectively, variables are drawn from the literature that are expected to have positive and negative relationships with the number of out-of-home placements experienced by youth in the sample.

Research Question 3: *Which sets of variables best explain out-of-home placements for African-American male delinquents?*

Hypothesis 5: An ecological set of variables including Age at Intake, Single Parent Family type, Adjudications, and Family Functioning will better explain Number of Placements than will blocks that contain demographics, offense history, clinical characteristics, or family characteristics alone.

Hypothesis 6: An ecological set of variables including Age at Intake, Felony Offenses, use of a Ventilation coping strategy, and Number of Prior Placements, will better explain Length of Stay in the most recent placement, than will blocks that contain demographics, offense history, clinical characteristics, family characteristics, or placement history alone.

Research Question 3 is directed toward testing the relative value of specified combinations of variables in explaining confinement. This part of the study extends the understanding provided by the correlations, and allows a focus on comparing blocks of variables to determine the degree to which they provide information about the experience of out-of-home placement. Multiple regression analysis was used to address this question.

Hypothesis 5 focuses on the outcome variable, Number of Placements. It specifies the expectation that a set of variables, which contains elements of various levels of the youth's ecological system, will better explain the phenomenon than any other set of variables which exist at a single level of the social ecology. The ecological perspective and the literature on delinquency were used to inform this hypothesis.

Hypothesis 6 centers on Length of Stay in the most recent placement as the outcome variable. It also specifies a set of ecological variables at multiple levels as a better explanation than sets of variables at single levels of the youth's social ecology.

Together, these research questions contributed to formulation of the research design. The hypotheses formed the basis for selection of the particular analytic techniques.

PSYCHOMETRICS OF CLINICAL INSTRUMENTS

The purpose of conducting confirmatory factor analyses of the published instruments that are typically used to measure stressors, coping, and family functioning, was to ensure valid and reliable measurement of the clinical constructs involved in the study. While the intent was not to challenge the work of those who developed these widely used instruments, it was noted that the samples used for development of these measures may have differed greatly from the participant population targeted by this study. An implicit set of hypotheses stipulated that a homogeneous sample of African-American delinquent youth in placement may have contact with different stressors, use different combinations of coping activities, and experience different patterns of family cohesion and control, than did the samples used for production of the original scales. The A-FILE used an initial sample of 30 youth from a suburban high school, and a subsequent sample described only as 500 junior and senior high school students (McCubbin & Patterson, 1991). Although three successive samples were used to develop the ACOPE scales, each of these samples was characterized as upper-middle to high socio-economic status (Patterson & McCubbin, 1991). The FACES II scales were constructed with "non-problem" families who were predominantly Lutheran and white (Fredman & Sherman, 1987). While previous work had established particular norms and cutting points for scoring these instruments for application to a "non-White" population (Grasso, 1985), it was deemed important to verify the latent variables contained in the instruments or to develop more appropriate scales if they were warranted. The results of the confirmatory factor analyses of the A-FILE, ACOPE, and FACES II are described in separate sections below.

A-FILE

Results of the confirmatory factor analysis for the A-FILE items, shown in Table 6, indicated that the scales included in the instrument were problematic in application to this sample. The published internal consistency reliabilities were noted to be relatively low (see Chapter 5), and none of the original scales had acceptable combinations of strength and significance of internal consistency, and significance of distinctiveness from other scales.

A review of Table 6 shows that the Transitions, Sexuality, Losses, Substance Use, and Legal Conflict scales did not possess acceptable internal consistency for this sample. For each of these scales, the alpha coefficient was below a predetermined cut-off of .70. Only Responsibilities and Strains had an acceptable coefficient alpha at .75, but this value was not significant at $p.>.05$, with a value of .000. This scale also proved to be unacceptable due to its lack of distinctiveness as indicated by the insignificance of its parallel Chi Square at .817 ($p<.05$). The Sexuality, and Losses scales had acceptable distinctiveness from other scales with significance values at .010 and .019, respectively, but were still rejected due to their observed problems with internal consistency. (The use of $p>.05$ for the internal consistency Chi Square, and distinctiveness in the form of parallelism are explained in end notes.)

The stressor measure was, thus, called into question. In line with the exploratory purpose of the study in relation to the specified sample, rather than broad generalization of findings or comparison to other populations, it was decided to use the existing items to construct new scales with acceptable psychometric properties in this application.

For the A-FILE, a complication to scale modification was introduced by a methodological issue regarding the construction of stressful event measurement scales. Clearly, the A-FILE items refer to stressful events or what fits into stress theory as "stressors" (Pearlin,

Table 6: Psychometrics of A-FILE Scales

Scale	Int Consist (alpha)	Int Consist Chi Square	df	p	Parallel Chi Square	df	P
Transitions	.50	115.671	90	.036	49.390	65	.925
Sexuality	.34	1.294	5	.936	30.507	15	.010
Losses	.44	46.751	20	.000	48.137	30	.019
Responsibilities and Strains	.75	246.237	170	.000	77.791	90	.817
Substance Use	.48	1.956	5	.855	19.959	15	.174
Legal Conflict	.04	N/A	-	-	5.601	2	.061
Family Tensions *	.71	35.620	27	.124	24.155	14	.044

* Family Tensions scale derived from A-FILE items for this sample.

N/A indicates that the scale had only two items, and it was not possible to calculate the internal consistency Chi Square value.

Significance (p) of internal consistency Chi Square is indicated by a value above .05 (because it tests for significant deviation from a unidimensional factor as explained in end notes).

Significance (p) of parallel Chi Square is indicated by a value below .05.

1989), but the fit of these events into scales could not be adequately accomplished by a statistical procedure alone. The developers of the A-FILE made explicit their decision to conceptually cluster the items, without the expectation that they be statistically related, into stressor categories (McCubbin & Patterson, 1991). The conceptual categories were submitted to confirmatory factor analysis to validate the scales, and assign factor loadings to the items, as reported in Chapter 5. The literature supports this position by noting that stressors do not necessarily cluster together in neat scales, because of the low frequency of serious stressors, such as loss by death (McCubbin & Patterson, 1983). Thus, the incidence of one stressor may not be correlated with the incidence of another stressor that would conceptually fall into the same category.

Other researchers have utilized an alternative strategy that applies weights to life events, which reflect the relative amount of change required by the individual to adapt to the circumstances of the event (Dohrenwend & Dohrenwend, 1978; Newcomb, Huba, & Bentler, 1986). Such a strategy is inappropriate for the purpose of the A-FILE as an inventory of life events. Moreover, it is also inappropriate for the present study which considers the presence or absence of stressors in relation to outcome variables rather than focusing concern on the degree of personal adaptation as a measured variable.

For this study, an approach similar to the one used for original A-FILE scale development was used. Once low quality items were removed as described in Chapter 5, the items were conceptually grouped into categories and then submitted to confirmatory factor analysis. One acceptable scale for stressors was developed from the A-FILE items. The emergent scale was named Family Tensions because it included items that centered on emotional and behavioral conflicts between family members (see Chapter 5 for a complete list of items and factor loadings). This scale exhibited acceptable psychometrics and was clearly discriminated from items in the instrument's original Losses and Transitions scales, which were used to test its distinctiveness. Family Tensions showed an internal consistency coefficient (alpha) of .71, significance of its internal consistency Chi Square value ($p > .05$), and significance of its parallel Chi Square value ($p < .05$). These characteristics are also shown in Table 6.

ACOPE

Results of the confirmatory factor analysis for the ACOPE items indicated that the scales included in the instrument did not adequately measure the identified constructs for this sample. Results of analysis of the ACOPE items alone (as shown in Table 7) indicated that only the Diversions scale showed acceptable combinations of strength and significance of internal consistency, and significance of distinctiveness. The internal consistency coefficient (alpha) for Diversions was .78 and significant at $p=.127$ ($p>.05$), as was its distinctiveness from the other ACOPE scales, indicated by the parallel Chi Square at $p=.000$ ($p<.05$).

The Ventilation, Solving Family Problems, and Demanding Activity scales also achieved acceptable alpha levels at .72, .77, and .77 respectively. Neither, however, showed significance ($p>.05$) of internal consistency with values of $p=.026$, $p=.013$, and $p=.000$, respectively. Ventilation attained significance ($p<.05$) of distinctiveness at $p=.006$. Solving Family Problems was just past the significance point at $p=.057$, and Demanding Activity was not significant at $p=.221$.

In addition, the Self-Reliance ($p=.000$), Social Support ($p=.003$), Avoiding ($p=.000$), and Relaxing ($p=.000$) scales showed significance ($p<.05$) of distinctiveness, but evidenced the noted problems with internal consistency.

The Close Friends, Professional Support, and Humor scales performed poorly in both internal consistency and distinctiveness. Close Friends showed an internal consistency coefficient (alpha) of .65, Professional Support achieved .35, and Humor .59. These scales had too few items to calculate the significance of these alpha values, which did not matter anyway due to their low coefficients. Significance of distinctiveness ($p<.05$) for each of these scales was not achieved with respective values of $p=.443$, $p=.170$, and $p=.380$.

Following this initial analysis, the A-FILE, ACOPE, and FACES II items were combined for confirmatory factor analysis of the stressor, coping, and family functioning constructs together, in order to further test the robustness of the scales and to guard against confounding of the clinical characteristics. Under these conditions, the Diversions scale performed differently, and only items from the Ventilation scale showed an acceptable combination of values. (One item, "Let off steam by complaining to friends", was dropped in the construction of

Table 7: Psychometrics of ACOPE Scales (part one)

Scale	Int Consist (alpha)	Int Consist Chi Square	df	p	Parallel Chi Square	df	p
Ventilation	.72	25.921	14	.026	85.125	55	.006
Diversions	.78	35.483	27	.127	134.639	77	.000
Self-Reliance	.61	25.134	14	.033	125.033	55	.000
Social Support	.69	10.320	14	.738	88.046	55	.003
Solving Family Problems	.77	28.342	14	.013	72.547	55	.057
Avoiding	.50	38.808	9	.000	122.182	44	.000
Spiritual Support	.67	0.000	2	-	25.246	22	.285

N/A indicates that the scale had only two items, and it was not possible to calculate the internal consistency Chi Square value.

Significance (*p*) of internal consistency Chi Square is indicated by a value above .05 (because it tests for significant deviation from a unidimensional factor as explained in end notes).

Significance (*p*) of parallel Chi Square is indicated by a value below .05.

Table 7: Psychometrics of ACOPE Scales (part two)

Scale	Int Consist (alpha)	Int Consist Chi Square	df	p	Parallel Chi Square	df	p
Close Friends	.65	N/A	-	-	11.006	11	.443
Professional Support	.35	N/A	-	-	15.291	11	.170
Demanding Activity	.77	18.668	5	.000	38.903	33	.221
Humor	.592	N/A	-	-	11.791	11	.380
Relaxing	.46	5.407	5	.368	90.492	33	.000
Ventilation *	.72	12.736	9	.175	23.745	8	.003
Personal Investment *	.82	16.100	20	.710	24.655	12	.017

* Ventilation and Personal Investment scales derived from ACOPE items for this sample. N/A indicates that the scale had only two items, and it was not possible to calculate the internal consistency Chi Square value.

Significance (p) of internal consistency Chi Square is indicated by a value above .05 (because it tests for significant deviation from a unidimensional factor as explained in end notes).

Significance (p) of parallel Chi Square is indicated by a value below .05.

the newly formed Ventilation scale.) In this analysis, Ventilation had an internal consistency coefficient (alpha) of .72, which was significant ($p>.05$) at $p=.175$, and showed significant distinctiveness ($p<.05$) at $p=.003$. Another acceptable scale emerged, which was named Personal Investment, to represent its combination of self-development and support for others. Results of the confirmatory factor analysis of the Ventilation and Personal Investment scales are shown in Table 7, along with the results of the analysis of the original scales. Items included in both scales and their factor loadings are listed in Chapter 5. The decision to better specify the measures for this sample was validated. For further analyses involving coping, only the newly formed Ventilation scale and the Personal Investment scale derived from the ACOPE items were used.

FACES II

An initial confirmatory factor analysis of the FACES II items alone indicated that the primary scales and subscales did not possess acceptable combinations of strength and significance of internal consistency, and significance of distinctiveness for this sample. These values are presented in Table 8.

The two primary scales, Adaptability and Cohesion, showed acceptable internal consistency coefficients (alphas), probably due to a relatively high number of items, but did not meet the significance test for internal consistency. Adaptability displayed an alpha of .74, $p=.001$ (significant at $p>.05$). Cohesion had an alpha of .78, $p=.000$. Both passed the test for significance of distinctiveness, with Adaptability at $p=.024$ and Cohesion at $p=.026$ (significant at $p<.05$).

The subscales of Adaptability include Assertiveness, Leadership, Discipline, Negotiation, Roles, and Rules. Due to the limited number of items in each subscale, it was not possible to calculate the significance of the internal consistency coefficient. Assertiveness ($p=.000$), Leadership ($p=.019$), and Discipline ($p=.005$) each achieved significance of distinctiveness ($p<.05$). Negotiation ($p=.944$), and Roles ($p=.106$) did not demonstrate significance of distinctiveness.

The subscales of Cohesion include Emotional Bonding, Family Boundaries, Coalitions, Time, Space, Friends, Decision-Making, and Interests/Recreation. None of these subscales achieved an acceptable

Table 8: Psychometrics of FACES II Scales (part one)

Scale	Int Consist (alpha)	Int Consist Chi Square	df	p	Parallel Chi Square	df	p
Adaptability	.74	138.408	90	.001	24.850	13	.024
Assertiveness	.28	.070	2	-	71.864	26	.000
Leadership	.35	N/A	-	-	24.286	12	.019
Discipline	.29	N/A	-	-	29.558	13	.005
Negotiation	.73	.000	2	-	15.667	26	.944
Roles	.47	N/A	-	-	19.570	13	.106
Rules	.18	N/A	-	-	18.457	13	.141

Adaptability is a primary scale of FACES II. Other scales are subscales of Adaptability. N/A indicates that the scale had only two items, and it was not possible to calculate the internal consistency Chi Square value.

Significance (p) of internal consistency Chi Square is indicated by a value above .05 (because it tests for significant deviation from a unidimensional factor as explained in end notes).

Significance (p) of parallel Chi Square is indicated by a value below .05.

Table 8: Psychometrics of FACES II Scales (part two)

Scale	Int Consist (alpha)	Int Consist Chi Square	df	p	Parallel Chi Square	df	p
Cohesion	.78	214.925	119	.000	27.322	15	.026
Emotional Bonding	.60	N/A	-	-	7.278	13	.887
Family Boundaries	.40	N/A	-	-	7.426	13	.879
Coalitions	.37	N/A	-	-	5.956	13	.948
Time	.54	N/A	-	-	31.101	13	.003
Space	.29	N/A	-	-	35.715	13	.000
Friends	.31	N/A	-	-	14.570	13	.335
Decision-Making	.35	N/A	-	-	10.072	13	.688
Interests/Recreation	.04	N/A	-	-	27.866	13	.009
Family Functioning	.87	90.938	77	.132	37.014	24	.044

Cohesion is a primary scale of the FACES II. Other scales are subscales of Cohesion.
Family Functioning is a new scale derived from FACES II Adaptability and Cohesion items.
N/A indicates that the scale had only two items, and it was not possible to calculate the internal consistency Chi Square value.
Significance (p) of internal consistency Chi Square is indicated by a value above .05 (because it tests for significant deviation from a unidimensional factor as explained in end notes).
Significance (p) of parallel Chi Square is indicated by a value below .05.

internal consistency coefficient. Emotional Bonding showed an internal consistency of .60, Family Boundaries .40, Coalitions.37,Time .54, Space .29, Friends .305, Decision-Making .35, and Interests/Recreation .04. In addition, neither of these subscales contained enough items to compute significance of their internal consistency coefficients. Only Time (p=.003), Space (p=.000), and Interests/Recreation (p=.009) demonstrated significance of distinctiveness ($p<.05$). Emotional Bonding (p=.887), Family Boundaries (p=.879), Coalitions (p=.948), Friends (p=.335), and Decision-Making (p=.688) each failed to achieve significance.

When the FACES II items were combined with the A-FILE and the ACOPE items to test the latent constructs, the significance of distinctiveness for both Adaptability and Cohesion disappeared. Therefore, items from both scales were combined to construct one scale of Family Functioning as described in Chapter 5, which was tested against items from the original A-FILE and the original ACOPE. Its psychometric properties were acceptable, as may be seen in Table 8. Family Functioning achieved an internal consistency coefficient (alpha) of .874, which was significant at p=.132 ($p>.05$). In addition, it showed significance of distinctiveness with a value of p=.044 ($p<.05$). The performance of this scale substantiated the decision to test and reconstruct the family clinical characteristics scales.

DESCRIPTION OF SAMPLE

The first research question focuses on a description of the sample. Hypothesis 1 specifies the combination of expected characteristics at the individual level. Hypothesis 2 is concerned with the sample being representative of the overall agency population of African-American males.

Research Question 1: What personal, family, and environmental characteristics describe African-American male delinquents who experience out-of-home placements?

To address this question generally, descriptive statistics for each of the selected variables were obtained. They include Age at Intake, Family Type, Urban Environment, Intake from Home, offense history (including Adjudications, Status Offenses, and Felony Offenses), Number of Prior Out-of-Home Placements, encounters with stressors (as Family Tensions), use of coping strategies (in the form of

Ventilation and Personal Investment), Family Functioning, Length of Stay, Type of Release from the agency program, and Aftercare Placement. The descriptive statistics obtained include frequencies and means for continuous variables, with standard deviations, and maximum and minimum values of the distributions. Frequencies and percentages for each level of the categorical variables were also computed.

Age at Intake is represented in Table 9. The youngest delinquent taken into this placement was not quite 13 years old, while the oldest was midway through his seventeenth year. These values reflect the rules governing juvenile justice in Michigan at the time, which set minimum and maximum ages for intake at 12 and 18, respectively. The average age of the sample is about 15.5 years old with a standard deviation of 1.04.

Table 9: Age at Intake

Age at Intake	12	13	14	15	16	17
Frequency	3	14	31	66	49	8
Percent	1.7	8.2	18.1	38.6	28.7	4.7

N = 171
Mean Age at Intake = 15.5 years (SD 1.04).

Family composition is shown in Table 10. Youth from single parent families predominated at 112, or 65.5%. The remaining participants totaled 37 (about 21.5%) from two parent nuclear families, 18 (10.5%) from extended families, two (about 1%) were adopted, and only another two (about 1%) came from foster families.

Table 10: Family Type

Family Type	Two Parent	Single Parent	Foster	Adoptive	Extended
Frequency	37	112	2	2	18
Percent	21.6	65.5	1.2	1.2	10.5

N = 171

As indicated in Table 11, which shows County of Intake by Urban and Non-Urban type, the vast majority of youth came from urban areas. This is especially true of the metropolitan Detroit area, with 105 from

Wayne county, 11 from Macomb county, and 4 from Oakland county, representing 70% of the sample. Counties within 50 miles of Detroit that serve as commuter bases include Lapeer and Livingston with five and six cases respectively, combining for about 6% of the total. Primarily urban counties, such as Genesee and Saginaw containing the large cities of Flint and Saginaw respectively, provided another 10.5 % of the cases, with ten from Flint and eight from Saginaw. The remainder of the youth came from obviously rural counties. They totaled 20 cases and about 13% of the sample.

Table 11: Urban and Rural Counties of Intake

	Urban County	Non-Urban County
Frequency	138	33
Percent	80.7	19.3

     N = 171

As indicated in Table 12, the bulk of these youth, 137 or 80%, came into placement directly from their family homes. The next largest subgroup, nine or just over 5%, came from private facilities such as other residential programs.

Table 12: Intake Living Situation

Intake Living Situation	Frequency	Percent
Home	137	80.1
Other Family Home	1	.6
Group Home	5	2.9
Jail	2	1.2
Youth Home (Detention)	6	3.5
Shelter	7	4.1
Private Facility (Residential Care)	9	5.3
State Institution	2	1.2
Other	1	.6
Missing Data	1	.6

     N = 171

Shelters used for child welfare cases contributed seven youth comprising about 4% of the cases. Restrictive programs provided the remainder of the cases, with six (3.5%) from county youth homes, five (about 3%) from group homes, two (1%) from a state institution, and two from county jail. Only one youth came from a family setting other than that indicated in his family type, and one case had missing data.

As shown in Table 13, the range of status offenses had a low value of zero and a high value of two. Only 21, or about 12% of the youth, committed two status offenses, while 44 (about 26%) had a record of one. The records of 106, or 62%, of the youth showed no status offenses. The mean number of status offenses is .50, with a standard deviation of .71.

Table 13: Status Offenses

Number of Status Offenses	0	1	2
Frequency	106	44	21
Percent	62	26	12

N = 171
Mean # of Status Offenses at Intake = .50 (SD .71)

Felony offenses are more numerous among the sample, as is apparent in Table 14. The average number of recorded felony offenses is 2.89 with a standard deviation of 2.45. The range of values reaches from zero to 13. Only three youth (less than 2%) committed felony offenses at the levels of 11, 12, and 13 each, while 28 (just over 16%) committed none. One felony offense was attributed to 29 youth, or 17%, of the sample. A sizable group committed two to five felonies. Twenty-seven youth (about 16%) committed two felonies and the same number committed three felonies. Four felonies were recorded for 28 youth or about 16%, and five felonies for 11 (just over 6% of the sample). The remainder of the youth committed from six to nine felonies, with six committed by six youth (3.5%), seven by seven youth (about 4%), eight by three youth (under 2%), and nine by two youth (just over 1%).

Table 14: Felony Offenses

Number of Felony Offenses	Frequency	Percent
0	28	16.4
1	29	17
2	27	15.8
3	27	15.8
4	28	16.4
5	11	6.4
6	6	3.5
7	7	4.1
8	3	1.8
9	2	1.2
10	0	0
11	1	.6
12	1	.6
13	1	.6

N = 171
Mean Number of Felony Offenses = 2.89 (SD 2.45)

Table 15 displays information about the adjudication record of youth in the sample. Involvement with the juvenile court is a necessary condition for out-of-home placement under normal circumstances, but five youth (almost 3% of the sample) showed no adjudications on their records. This is probably explained by the fact that a case originally classed as a child welfare case, could be "escalated" in placement if the youth's behavior becomes troublesome in the opinion of the case worker. Thus, the initial basis for out-of-home placement is provided by child protection laws, but the child undergoes *de facto* categorization as a delinquent. Most youth had records of one to four adjudications, with a notable drop in frequency above that point. Fifty-three, or 31%, had one adjudication, 48 (about 28%) had two, 29 (17%) had three, and 20 (almost 12%) had four. Four youth, or about 2%, had five adjudications each, the same number had six, and three had seven adjudications. One youth each showed adjudications at the levels of 9, 10, 11, 15, and 16. The average number of adjudications was 2.58, with a standard deviation of 2.25.

Table 15: Adjudications

Number of Adjudications	Frequency	Percent
0	5	2.9
1	53	31.0
2	48	28.1
3	29	17.0
4	20	11.7
5	4	2.3
6	4	2.3
7	3	1.8
8	0	0
9	1	.6
10	1	.6
11	1	.6
12	0	0
13	0	0
14	0	0
15	1	.6
16	1	.6

N = 171
Mean Number of Adjudications = 2.58 (SD 2.25)

The previous placement data, in Table 16, show that only 39, or about 23%, of the youth had not been placed out-of-the-home prior to agency intake. The bulk of the cases were clustered between one and five inclusive. Thirty youth (17.5%) had been in one placement, and the same number had two placements. Thirty-six (about 21%) were placed out of the home three times prior, 13 (about 7.5%) had four prior placements, and nine (about 5%) had been in five prior placements. Three youth (less than 2%) had been in six placements, four youth (just over 2%) were placed seven times, three youth placed eight times, and two placed ten times. One youth was placed out of the home 12 times, and one exceptional case showed 21 prior out-of-home placements. Using these data, the mean number of out-of-home placements was 2.44, with a standard deviation of 2.62.

Table 16: Prior Placements

Number of Prior Placements	Frequency	Percent
0	39	22.8
1	30	17.5
2	30	17.5
3	36	21.1
4	13	7.6
5	9	5.3
6	3	1.8
7	4	2.3
8	3	1.8
9	0	0
10	2	1.2
11	0	0
12	1	.6
21	1	.6

N = 171
Mean Number of Prior Placements = 2.44 (SD 2.62)

A total of 102 youth, or about 60%, had experienced two or more out-of-home placements prior to the most recent agency entry. With the addition of cases where there was one placement prior to this agency intake, the total number of youth with multiple placements (including the most recent placement) rises to 132. This comprises 77% of the sample.

Encounter with stressors is represented in the form of Family Tensions. As may be seen in Table 17, for Family Tensions, youth responded with a range of scores from one through eight events over the 12 months immediately preceding placement. The average was just over five, with a standard deviation of about two. Most youth were clearly clustered in the upper range of the distribution. Twenty-eight (over 26%) reported eight stressors, 30 (17.5%) identified seven, 24 (14%) noted six, and another 30 listed five events. The remainder showed one to four events, with seven (about 4%) indicating one Family Tension stressor, 20 (almost 12%) reporting two, and 16 (about 9.5%) each reporting three and four stressful events.

Clearly, the youth in the sample experienced high levels of contact with stressors. These data are particularly striking when one recalls that Family Tensions represents only one form of stressor within a social ecology that potentially consists of many others.

Table 17: Family Tensions

Number of Family Tensions	Frequency	Percent
0	0	0
1	7	4.1
2	20	11.7
3	16	9.4
4	16	9.4
5	30	17.4
6	24	14
7	30	17.5
8	28	16.4

N = 171
Mean Number of Family Tensions Stressors = 5.19 (SD 2.12)

Use of coping strategies was assessed with the Personal Investment and Ventilation scales. The range of scores for Personal Investment, spans from one to five. The average score was 3.36, with a standard deviation of .84. Ventilation showed a range from one to five, with a mean of 2.74 and a standard deviation of .80. These values indicate that both forms of coping are often used by youth in this sample.

In order to test for a preference of one coping strategy over the other, a Coping Difference score was computed by obtaining standardized scores (z scores) for Personal Investment and Ventilation, and then subtracting each participant's Ventilation score from his Personal Investment score. Using scores above zero to represent youth who preferred Personal Investment coping to Ventilation coping, 84 cases were counted. Eighty-seven youth preferred Ventilation coping, when scores less than or equal to zero were counted.

Results for the Family Functioning scale showed a range of scores from 1.23 to 4.54, with a mean of 3.10 and a standard deviation of .64. These scores represent a moderate level of family cohesion and control.

Table 18: Length of Stay

LOS in Months	Frequency	Percent
1	4	2.3
2	0	0
3	3	1.8
4	3	1.8
5	4	2.3
6	6	3.5
7	1	.6
8	2	1.2
9	8	4.7
10	6	3.5
11	4	2.3
12	16	9.4
13	3	1.8
14	13	7.6
15	9	5.3
16	16	9.4
17	14	8.2
18	5	2.9
19	8	4.7
20	9	5.3
21	8	4.7
22	9	5.3
23	2	1.2
24	4	2.3
25	3	1.8
26	4	2.3
27	2	1.2
28	2	1.2
29	1	.6
30	0	0
31	1	.6
32	1	.6

N = 171 Mean Length of Stay in Months = 15.4 (SD 6.50)

Table 18 shows length of stay in the most recent agency placement rounded to the nearest month. Stays ranged from a low of less than one month (.73) to a high of 32 months. The mean was almost 15 and one-half months, with a standard deviation of 6.50.

Completion of treatment goals is displayed in Table 19. It shows that 11 youth (about 6.5 %) completed all goals, 49 (about 29%) Most, 76 (over 44%) Some, 23 (13.5%) None, and 12 (7%) Not Applicable. This category would be used for cases where discharge occurred too soon for the initial assessment and formal treatment planning conference to be completed, which was required within the first 30 days of placement. Summing the percentages for the All and Most categories shows that only about 35% of the youth successfully completed their treatment goals. The Not Applicable category would be most appropriate when a youth unlawfully left the agency site and was subsequently placed somewhere else, or when there was a court-ordered removal from the placement for unspecified reasons.

Table 19: Completion of Treatment Goals

Completion of Treatment Goals	Frequency	Percent
All	11	6.4
Most	49	28.7
Some	76	44.4
None	23	13.5
Not Applicable	12	7.0

N = 171

Despite the limited completion of treatment goals, release type indicates that most youth in the sample were satisfactorily released from the program. This is based on the categories of Agency Release and Administrative Release (as defined in Chapter 5). As shown in Table 20, Agency Release was reported for 61 youth (almost 36%) and Administrative Release included 40 youth (over 23%) for a total of about 59%. The remaining categories may be seen as unsatisfactory discharges. Administrative Discharge accounted for 29 youth (17%), Administrative Termination 25 (about 14.5%), Court Termination 12 (7%), State Termination three (less than 2%), and only one youth was discharged due to Inactive status.

Table 20: Type of Release

Type of Release	Frequency	Percent
Agency Release*	61	35.7
Administrative Release*	40	23.4
Administrative Discharge	29	17.0
Administrative Termination	25	14.6
Court Termination	12	7.0
State Termination	3	1.8
Inactive	1	.6

N = 171

* Agency Release and Administrative Release are counted as
successful release types, all others are unsuccessful.

Table 21: Placement Destination at Release

Placement Destination at Release	Frequency	Percent
Parent's Home	82	48.0
Relative's Home	12	7.0
Foster Home	12	7.0
Private Residential Facility	2	1.2
Group Home	14	8.2
County Residential Facility	1	.6
State Institution	11	6.4
Independent Living	7	4.1
Armed Services	1	.6
Non-Secure Shelter	7	4.1
Unknown	22	12.9

N = 171

As may be seen in Table 21, post placement destination data show that
upon release, 82 or 48% of the youth returned to their parent's home,
12 (7%) went to live with a relative, seven (about 4%) started
independent living, and one entered the Armed Services. Together,
these post placement destinations comprise settings that may be
considered to be unconfined. Although these youth were placed at
home immediately upon release, there is no data here to illuminate the
duration of their stay at home. The placement of 22 (almost 13%) was

unknown, which is most likely due to a termination of placement while the youth was not physically present in the placement. The others were placed in other out-of-home placements. Fourteen (about 8%) entered a group home program, 11 (about 6.5%) were sent to a state institution, 12 (7%) entered specialized foster care which is heavily supervised, two (about 1%) went to a private residential program, and one entered a county residential program. The remaining seven (about 4%) went to a non-secure shelter. These descriptive data were used to address the hypotheses stated under Research Question 1.

Hypothesis 1: The typical African-American male placed out-of-the home will be approximately sixteen years old, from a single-parent family, living in an urban environment, and will have been adjudicated for more than one delinquent offense.

Hypothesis 1 is supported by the data. The typical African-American male delinquent in this sample is 15.5 years old. He comes from a single parent family and resides in the Detroit metropolitan area. His illegal behavior seems to have escalated rapidly. He has either not engaged in minor juvenile infractions, or else has been able to elude court attention for them, as his formal record shows no pattern of status offenses. He has, however, been apprehended for serious crimes. His juvenile record includes three felony crimes against persons or property and he has been petitioned by the juvenile court and found to be delinquent three times. He came into the most recent placement directly from his home, but he has been placed elsewhere on two prior occasions.

He experiences a significant amount of family tension involving arguments with his parent over many of his personal choices including friends, dress, use of time, and involvement in activities. To cope with these and other sources of stress, he uses active problem solving methods to develop himself and help others, but also resorts to yelling, swearing, and threatening others when he gets upset. His family usually operates with moderate levels of emotional closeness and parental monitoring of his actions, but there may be fluctuations in these functions under difficult conditions.

He will stay in this placement well over a year. During that time, he will be expected to make progress toward treatment goals that are established by his staff team, but will perform only moderately well and achieve only some of what was set out for him. Nonetheless, he will be satisfactorily discharged from the facility and will return to his parent's home.

Hypothesis 2: This sample does not significantly differ from the agency population in age, offense history, or placement history.

Because one important criterion for sample selection was completion of all the clinical assessment instruments, it was deemed valuable to test whether this sample significantly differed on key attributes from youth admitted to the agency that did not complete the clinical instruments.

To test this hypothesis, the means of the sample for age at intake, adjudications, status offenses, felony offenses, and the number of previous placements were compared with all other agency cases that met the conditions of race, gender, and intake during the same years as the sample. The only known difference between these groups was that the research sample had completed all clinical assessment instruments. The overall population numbered 1742 youth after the research sample was removed. The means of the sample were compared with the means of the population using a one sample *t*-test, with results shown in Table 22.

Mean age at intake for the sample was 15.49 years, and for the population it was 15.86 years. This difference (.37) amounts to only about four and a half months, but it is statistically significant (*p*=.000). It should be noted, however, that for most clinical purposes, this difference in age is probably not relevant.

Offense history showed mixed results. The mean number of Status Offenses for the sample was .50 and the agency population value was .40. The difference of .10 was not significant (*p*=.058). Felony Offenses showed a mean of 2.89 for the sample against 1.35 for the population. Intuitively, this difference of an average of one and a half felonies appears to be an important difference, and the *t*-test for this variable showed it to be significant (*p*=.000). Number of Adjudications showed a sample mean of 2.58, with the agency group value at 1.94. This difference is statistically significant (*p*= .000).

Number of Prior Placements indicated a non-significant difference between the means (*p*=.106). The sample mean stands at 2.44 and the population mean at 2.77.

Table 22: Comparison of Study Sample with Agency Population
(African-American Males Admitted in Same Years)

Variable	Sample Mean	Agency Mean	t	df	p
Age at Intake	15.49	15.86	-4.66	170	.000
Status Offenses	.50	.40	1.10	170	.058
Felony Offenses	2.89	1.35	8.20	170	.000
Adjudications	2.58	1.94	3.75	170	.000
Prior Placements	2.44	2.77	-1.63	170	.106

Sample n = 171
Population N = 1742

It appears from this analysis, that the study sample, (those who completed the full set of clinical instruments) differs in some ways from the rest of the agency population of African-American males. The difference in age is notable, but not appreciable. The similarity in both status offense history and placement experience, indicate parity of the sample and the population. The significant differences in adjudications and serious criminal behavior, however, indicate that the sample may present an even greater risk to the community than the rest of the agency population, and that these youth may be at even higher risk for continued out-of-home placement.

CORRELATIONAL ANALYSIS

Research Question 2: What are the observed associations of personal, family, and environmental variables for African-American male delinquents who experience out-of-home placements?

This question was addressed by computing the Pearson Product-Moment correlations between each pair of included variables. Table 23 presents the correlations, showing two-tailed significance at $p \leq .01$ (**) and at $p \leq .05$ (*), in a diagonal matrix format. As is apparent from this matrix, even though several correlations are significant, the effect sizes are relatively low. Nonetheless, meaningful relationships among the variables may be identified. They are presented here, and discussed further in the section dealing with the correlational schematic, and in Chapter 7.

The older the youth at intake, the more felony offenses he is likely to have on his record. Younger delinquents are more likely to come from single parent families, and have shorter stays in placement than older youth. An adolescent from a single parent family is also more likely to experience a greater number of out-of-home placements throughout his delinquent career. Earning a successful release from the program is less likely for youth whose families live in cities. Those with fewer adjudications are more likely to come into placement directly from their families' homes rather than from another placement.

Felony offenders with long criminal records are not as likely to stay a long time in this placement as compared to those with fewer felony offenses. Youth with higher numbers of prior placements tend to perceive higher levels of family functioning as well. The youth with more placements are not likely to stay a lengthy period in this one, but they will also probably not complete many of their treatment goals.

A high number of stressors in the family is associated with a likelihood that the youth will use a coping style that ventilates his emotions, and that he will probably not return to his family home upon release from the program. Use of a ventilation coping strategy means there is less chance that a youth will engage in personal investment types of coping, but also that he will have a better chance of going home when he leaves the agency.

Higher levels of family functioning are associated with higher numbers of out-of-home placements, but the reader should be especially cautious about judging the direction of this effect. Possible explanations are considered in the section dealing with the correlational schematic.

Longer stays in placement are linked to a successful release and returning to one's family home. Perhaps not surprisingly, a successful release from the program is associated with the opportunity to return home.

Hypothesis 3: Number of Placements will be significantly and positively correlated with Age at Intake, Status Offenses, Felony Offenses, Adjudications, Family Tensions, and the Ventilation coping strategy.

Table 23: Correlation Matrix of Ecological Variables (part one)

	Age	Single Parent	Urban	Home Intake	Status	Felony	Adjudication	Prior Placement	Family Tensions
Age									
Single Parent	-.15*								
Urban	.11	.08							
Home Intake	.05	-.04	.061						
Status	-.10	.10	-.07	.14					
Felony	.23*	.08	.00	.08	-.09				
Adjudication	-.02	-.06	.04	-.15*	-.09	.01			
Prior Placement	-.06	.16*	-.03	.01	-.02	-.02	.05		
Family Tensions	.07	.02	.09	-.03	.00	.05	.05	-.03	

* significant at *p*<.05   ** significant at *p*<.01

Table 23: Correlation Matrix of Ecological Variables (part two)

	Age	Single Parent	Urban	Home Intake	Status	Felony	Adjudication	Prior Placement	Family Tensions
Personal Investment	.03	-.09	.02	.12	-.04	-.03	-.03	.03	.11
Ventilation	.09	.00	.05	.05	-.03	-.05	.04	.01	-.29**
Family Functioning	-.04	-.11	.00	-.04	-.03	-.11	-.01	.17*	.05
LOS	-.25**	-.03	.06	.08	-.09	-.18*	-.02	-.17*	-.07
Successful Goals	.03	.08	-.01	-.04	-.02	.06	-.04	-.18*	.01
Successful Release	-.07	-.05	-.20*	-.05	-.15	-.10	.05	-.04	-.10
Aftercare Home	.09	-.12	.14	.17*	-.12	-.06	-.06	-.01	-.15*
Number of Placements	-.06	.16*	-.03	.01	-.02	-.02	.05	x	.08
Total Placements	-.08	.20*	-06	-.06	-.02	.00	.06	x	.11

* significant at $p < .05$ ** significant at $p < .01$

x Total Placements is computed by adding one to Number of Placements, so a correlation would be meaningless.

Table 23: Correlation Matrix of Ecological Variables (part three)

	Personal Investment	Ventilation	Family Function	LOS	Success Goals	Success Release	Aftercare Home	# Plcmnts	Total Plcmnts
Personal Investment									
Ventilation	-.20**								
Family Function	.17*	-.12							
LOS	.06	.02	-.04						
Success Goals	-.13	.08	-.03	-.02					
Success Release	-.05	.10	-.11	.46**	-.04				
Aftercare Home	.05	.18*	.09	.19*	-.02	.33**			
# Plcmnts	.03	.01	.17*	-.17*	-.18*	-.04	-.01		
Total Plcmnts	.03	-.04	.14	-.20*	-.15*	-.11	-.28**	x	

* significant at *p*<.05   ** significant at *p*<.01
x Total Placements is computed by adding one to Number of Placements, so a correlation would be meaningless.

This hypothesis was stated in a compound fashion to simplify presentation. Actually, the correlation of each variable with Number of Placements is considered separately.

Number of Placements is not significantly correlated with any of the variables named in this hypothesis using a one-tailed test. Its correlation and level of significance with Age at Intake is r= -.059, p=.223; Status Offenses r = -.024, p= .379; Felony Offenses r= -.022, p= .387; Adjudications r= .046, p= .276; Family Tensions r= .079, p= .154; Ventilation r= .012, p= .440. Due to the weak effect sizes, as well as the failure to pass the significance level, this hypothesis is not supported.

Hypothesis 4: Number of Placements will be significantly and negatively correlated with use of the Personal Investment coping strategy and Family Functioning.

Again, this hypothesis was stated in a compound fashion to simplify presentation. The correlation of each variable with Number of Placements is considered separately.

Number of Placements is neither negatively correlated with Personal Investment nor Family Functioning using a one-tailed test at the p=.05 level. Rather, it is positively and significantly correlated with Family Functioning r= .166, p= .015. Its values for Personal Investment are r= .026, p= .366. Due to the inverse of the predicted valence of the association between Number of Placements and Family Functioning, as well as the weak effect size and failure to pass the level of significance of the association between Number of Placements and Personal Investment, this hypothesis is not supported.

Number of Placements is significantly correlated, however, with other included variables, using a two-tailed test at the p<.05 level. Its correlations with Single Parent Family (r= .156, p= .041); with Length of Stay (r= -.171, p= .025); and with Successful Program Completion (r= -.182, p= .017) are described in the explanation of the correlation matrix above.

The need to reject this hypothesis could stem from a cycle of repeated placements. These results may reflect the impacts of one or more out-of-home placements on variables that would normally be expected to lead to out-of-home placements. For example, prior placements may have had a positive impact on family functioning through treatment efforts, or due to stabilization of delinquent behavior through external control.

The association of out-of-home placements with variables not included in the hypothesis shows that the relationship with family composition may remain relatively constant across the span of placements. Prior experience with out-of-home placements, however, may allow the learning of skills that reduce length of stay, but do not significantly affect completion of all treatment goals.

SCHEMATICS OF CORRELATIONS

Research Question 3: Which sets of variables best explain out-of-home placements for African-American male delinquents?

This question was partially addressed by the construction of a set of schematics, which show selected linkages of variables leading to Total Out-of-Home Placements. The linkages are based on the observed correlations presented above, but each diagram shows only one set of linkages, rather than complicating the picture with all the observed relationships. No correlation values are included because the intent of these diagrams is only to help the reader visualize the connections. The valences (negative or positive) of the observed correlations are presented to indicate the direction of influence that the variables exert on each other within the sequence.

Each schematic is organized in the same way, with the only difference being the particular linkage shown. In each schematic, the variables are organized in columns that show their order in time. The first column consists of Demographic variables, which include Age at Intake, Single Parent Family Type, Urban Environment, and Intake from Home. The second column is Offense History, which includes Felony Offenses, Adjudications, and Prior Placements. Clinical Characteristics come next. This column includes Family Functioning, Family Tensions Stressors, Personal Investment Coping, and Ventilation Coping. Program Variables include Length of Stay, Successful Program Completion, and Successful Release. The Aftercare level is captured by Aftercare Placement Home. Total Out-of-Home Placements is the outcome variable.

In accord with the goals of this study, compound linkages involving Total Out-of-Home Placements are considered below. The reader is invited to track the linkages from level to level, in order to identify potential causal chains. Interpretations of each diagram may be based on the direction of the arrows and the signs (+/-) of the connections.

In Figure 5, one compound connection traces the linkage from Age at Intake through Felony Offenses, Length of Stay, Successful Release, and Aftercare Placement Home to Total Out-of-Home Placements. Age at Intake also has a direct negative effect on Length of Stay, which, in turn, exerts a direct negative effect on Total Out-of-Home Placements. Age at Intake is also shown as having mutual influence with Single Parent Family Type. According to these connections, Age at Intake increases the likelihood that the youth will have accumulated a record of felony offenses, and it directly limits Length of Stay.

Having a record of felonies, however, decreases length of stay in the most recent placement and increases the chance of successful release, which increases the likelihood of returning home upon release, and decreases the likelihood of additional out-of-home placements. This set of linkages shows that although being older at intake is associated with a higher number of recorded criminal offenses, the duration of confinement is not extended by such a criminal history. The inverse effect of age may be partially due to legal limits on confinement for youth who have reached age 19. Longer stays in placement, however, are more likely to be rewarded with an approved release and an attendant return to a home setting, rather than an additional out-of-home placement. Longer stays also serve to limit the accumulation of further out-of-home placements directly. Simply put, the youth cannot be placed into a different setting when he is maintained in the current one.

Shown in Figure 6, another important set of linkages goes from Single Parent Family type through Prior Placements, Family Functioning, Personal Investment, Ventilation, and Aftercare Placement Home, to Total Out-of-Home Placements. This set of connections, as well as a direct connection between Single Parent Family type and Total Out-of-Home Placements, shows that coming from a single parent family increases the likelihood of out-of-home

Figure 5: Schematic of Correlations (Age at Intake)

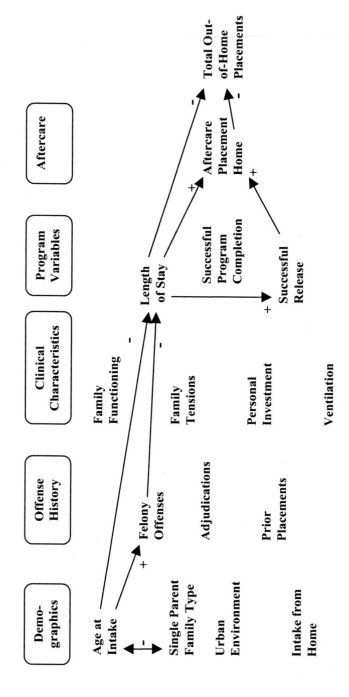

Figure 6: Schematic of Correlations (Single Parent Family Type)

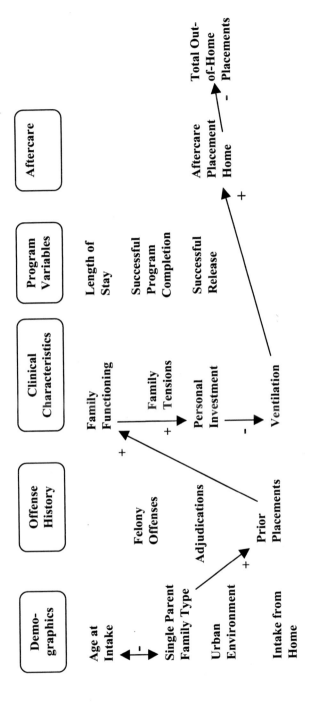

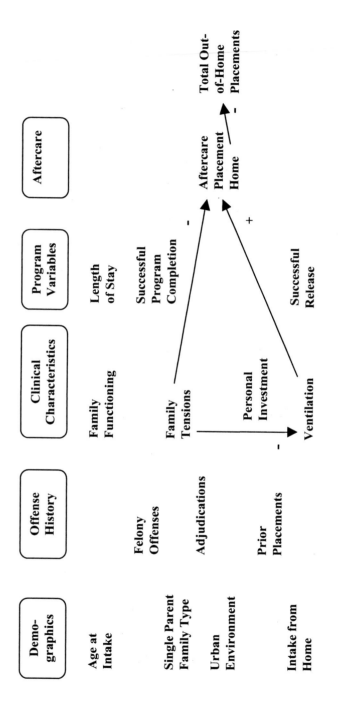

Figure 7: Schematic of Correlations (Family Tensions)

Figure 8: Schematic of Correlations (Urban Environment/Intake from Home)

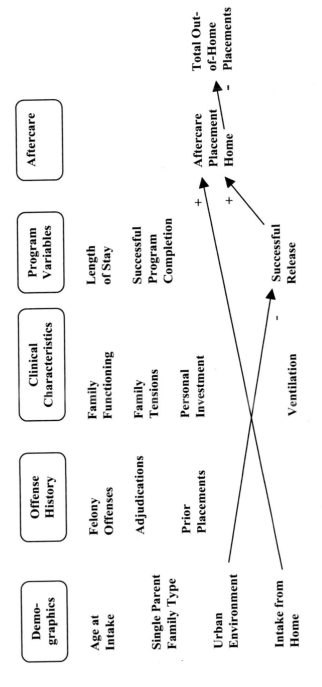

placement for sample youth. Entry into placement increases levels of family functioning in the areas of cohesion and control, as well as the adolescent's application of personal investment coping strategies. This would appear to indicate that two common targets of delinquency intervention programs are effectively addressed. Although personal investment and ventilation coping strategies are incompatible, ventilation increases the chances of placement at home and thereby decreases the addition of another out-of-home placement.

Figure 7 shows an additional notable linkage, which connects Family Tensions through Ventilation and Aftercare Placement Home to Total Out-of-Home Placements. Family Tensions also exerts a direct effect on Aftercare Placement Home. Although not conceptualized as an exogenous variable, Family Tensions represents a powerful stressor for the sample that has no significant identified inputs. This linkage highlights the importance of stress and coping factors in placement decisions, even though they are not directly linked to criminal or legal involvements.

Two other sets of connections are shown in Figure 8. They have fewer linkages, but are also relevant to understanding out-of-home placement. Coming from an urban environment directly decreases the likelihood of earning a successful release from the program, the granting of which would increase the potential for a home placement, instead of an out-of-home placement after release. Coming into placement from a home setting, however, directly increases the potential for a home placement at the end of the program, thereby preventing an additional out-of-home placement. These two connections illuminate the impact of the youth's home environment on placement decisions, and the value of maintaining them in home settings as a means of limiting the cycle of confinement.

Multiple Regression Analysis of Out-of-Home Placements

Research Question 3: Which sets of variables best explain out-of-home placements for African-American male delinquents?

This question was addressed by focusing on two dependent variables that represent forms of out-of-home placement. Simultaneous Multiple Regression was used to test models focused on Number of Placements, and Length of Stay in the most recent placement, as dependent variables. The following hypotheses specify the dependent variables and the blocks that are expected to best explain them, using the available data in standard multiple regression. By independent variable, the models are tested for significance, and compared with each other to determine greatest explanatory value based on greatest percentage of variance explained.

Because a standard multiple regression technique was used, it is important to remember that the independent variables would perform differently in other combinations. Conclusions should not be drawn regarding the importance of an individual variable outside the context of the specific model in which it was tested. In the following presentation, the contributions of the independent variables are evaluated only as they compare with one another within their respective block.

> *Hypothesis 5: An ecological set of variables including age at intake, single parent family type, adjudications, and family functioning will better explain Number of Placements, than will blocks that contain demographics, offense history, clinical characteristics, or family characteristics alone.*

This hypothesis is intended to test the relative value of the models as they compare to one another. While other combinations may come to mind for the reader, it should be noted that the intent was not to test all possible constructions, but rather to compare the explanatory value of various systems levels by themselves, with a more integrated systemic view. These models, therefore, were constructed as representations of systemic levels in the social ecology of the sample youth. The ecological model employed here includes variables from successive system levels in order to evaluate the additional understanding that an ecological approach purportedly allows.

The specific variables selected for inclusion in the ecological model were chosen on the basis of explicit rationales. Age at Intake was included because older youth have greater exposure to accumulation of out-of-home placements than do younger adolescents. Single Parent Families have been identified in the literature as having higher incidences of delinquency in their children (Minuchin, Montalvo, Guerney, & Rosman, 1967; Benson & Roehlkepartain, 1993; Kapp,

McCubbin, & Thompson 1993; Whittaker, Tripodi, & Grasso, 1993). Adjudications are used to represent a juvenile justice system intervention that is based on a formal recognition of the youth's delinquent behavior. The family functions of cohesion and control embedded in the Family Functioning variable are shown in the literature to be high correlates of delinquent behavior.

The predictive power of each model is indicated by the Adjusted R Square value, which estimates the percentage of variance explained by the model. Higher values indicate better predictive value. To assure confidence in accepting the model, each Adjusted R Square value is tested for significance ($p<.05$). In addition, the relative contribution of each variable within the block may be compared. These contributions are indicated by the standardized beta values for each individual variable. Higher betas indicate a more valuable contribution, assuming that the value was found to be significant.

Model 1, shown in Table 24, uses demographic variables including Urban Environment, Single Parent Family, and Age at Intake to explain Number of Placements. This model explains only about 1% of the variance (Adjusted R Square = .013), and fails to achieve significance (F=1.735, $p=$ .162). Only Single Parent Family (*beta*= .167, *t*= 2.157, $p=.032$) made a significant contribution to explanation of Number of Placements within this model. Age at Intake (*beta* = -.030, *t*= -.385, $p=.701$) and Urban Environment (*beta* = -.012, *t*= -.160, $p=.873$) were not useful variables in this analysis.

Table 24: Demographic Regression Model for Number of Placements

R	R Square	Adjusted R Square	Standard Error
.174	.030	.013	2.602

	Sum of Squares	*df*	Mean Square	F	Signif
Regression	35.249	3	11.750	1.735	.162
Residual	12.850	167	.008		
Total	13.459	170			

	Unstnd Beta	Stnd Error	Stnd Beta	*t*	Signif
Constant	4.073	3.063		1.330	.185
Age at Intake	-.008	.195	-.030	-.385	.701
Single Parent	.918	.426	.167	2.157	.032
Urban Envir	-.008	.510	-.012	-.160	.873

Model 2, shown in Table 25, is composed of offense history variables. It includes Status Offenses, Felony Offenses, Adjudications, and Intake from Home. Model 2 performs worse than Model 1 in explaining the variance of Number of Placements (Adjusted R Square = -.003) and also fails to show significance (p= .483). The contributions of the separate variables within this model have little value for understanding Number of Placements. Status Offenses shows a *beta* of -.062 (t= -.789, p=.431), Felony Offenses *beta* = -.025 (t= -.326, p=.745), Adjudications Beta = .121 (t=1.551, p=.123), and Intake from Home *beta* = .055 (t=.694, p=.489).

Table 25: Offense and Placement History Regression Model for Number of Placements

R	R Square	Adjusted R Square	Standard Error
.143	.021	-.003	2.623

	Sum of Squares	*df*	Mean Square	F	Signif
Regression	23.952	4	5.988	.870	.483
Residual	1142.270	166	6.881		
Total	1166.222	170			

	Unstnd Beta	Stnd Error	Stnd Beta	*t*	Signif
Constant	2.981	.593		5.029	.000
Status Offs	-.229	.291	-.062	-.789	.431
Felony Offs	-.003	.083	-.025	-.326	.745
Adjudications	.141	.091	.121	1.551	.123
Intake Home	.361	.520	.055	.694	.489

Model 3 (Table 26) focuses on the clinical characteristics of the youth, and includes Family Tensions (stressor), Personal Investment and Ventilation (coping strategies), and Family Functioning. The model explains only about 1% of the variance in number of placements (Adjusted R Square = .010), and is not significant (p=.226). Family Functioning is the individual variable in this block that performs the best as a predictor (*beta*= .166, t=2.143, p=.034). Family Tensions (*beta*= .052, t= .650, p=.517), Personal Investment (*beta*= .018, t= .228, p= .820), and Ventilation (*beta*= .082, t= 1.002, p=.318) all serve as poor predictors within this combination.

Table 26: Clinical Characteristics Regression Model for Number of Placements

R	R Square	Adjusted R Square	Standard Error
.183	.033	.010	2.606

	Sum of Squares	df	Mean Square	F	Signif
Regression	38.869	4	9.717	1.431	.226
Residual	1127.353	166	6.791		
Total	1166.222	170			

	Unstnd Beta	Stnd Error	Stnd Beta	t	Signif
Constant	.008	1.644		.050	.960
Fam Tensions	.006	.099	.052	.650	.517
Pers Investm	.006	.246	.018	.228	.820
Ventilation	.266	.266	.082	1.002	.318
Fam Functng	.681	.318	.166	2.143	.034

Model 4 (Table 27) enters the family characteristics of the youth as a block, and includes Single Parent Family, Family Tensions, and Family Functioning. The model achieves significance (p=.012), while explaining about 5% of the variance (Adjusted R Square = .046). Thus, family characteristics for this sample are a better predictor of number of placements than are demographics or offense history. Family Tensions

is the least productive element of this block (*beta* = .025, *t*=.331, *p*=.741), while Family Functioning (*beta* = .309, *t*=2.411, *p*= .017) and Single Parent Family (*beta* = .414, *t*=2.525, *p*=.013) better explain number of placements in this construction.

Table 27: Family Characteristics Regression Model for Number of Placements

R	R Square	Adjusted R Square	Standard Error
.251	.063	.046	2.558

	Sum of Squares	*df*	Mean Square	F	Signif
Regression	73.413	3	24.471	3.740	.012
Residual	1092.810	167	6.544		
Total	1166.222	170			

	Unstnd Beta	Stnd Error	Stnd Beta	*t*	Signif
Constant	.297	1.121		.265	.791
Single Parent	1.041	.414	.190	2.515	.013
Fam Tensions	.031	.093	.025	.331	.741
Fam Functng	.744	.309	.182	2.411	.017

Model 5 (Table 28) uses an ecological set of independent variables in an effort to explain the variance in number of placements. As noted above, this ecological set uses Age at Intake, Single Parent Family, Family Functioning, and Adjudications, to represent successive levels of the youth's environment. It is significant at the *p*=.006 level, and explains about 6% of the variance of number of placements (Adjusted R Square = .061). Although its explanatory value is quite low, it still performs as a better predictor than any of the other models constructed for this dependent variable. In this model, Single Parent Family and Family Functioning have about equal value as predictors (*beta* = .198, *t*=2.606, *p*=.010; *beta* = .191, *t*= 2.543, *p*= .012, respectively), while Adjudications (*beta* = .142, *t*=1.907, *p*=.058) and Age at Intake (*beta* = -.015, *t*= -.201, *p*=.841) perform less well.

Table 28: Ecological Regression Model for Number of Placements

R	R Square	Adjusted R Square	Standard Error
.288	.083	.061	2.538

	Sum of Squares	df	Mean Square	F	Signif
Regression	96.621	4	24.155	3.749	.006
Residual	1069.601	166	6.443		
Total	1166.222	170			

	Unstnd Beta	Stnd Error	Stnd Beta	t	Signif
Constant	.476	3.229		.147	.883
Age at Intake	-.004	.189	-.015	-.201	.841
Single Parent	1.087	.417	.195	2.606	.010
Adjudications	.166	.087	.142	1.907	.058
Fam Functng	.780	.307	.191	2.543	.012

Table 29: Summary of Regression Models for Number of Placements

Model	R	R Square	Adjusted R Square	Signif
Demographic	.174	.030	.013	.162
Offense History	.143	.021	-.003	.483
Clinical Characteristics	.183	.033	.010	.226
Family Characteristics	.251	.063	.046	.012
Ecological	.288	.083	.061	.006

The results of the regression models for Number of Placements are summarized in Table 29 to ease comparison. The ecological model (Model 5) performed better than the other four models in explaining variance while meeting an appropriate level of significance. Only the

Family Characteristics Model and the Ecological Model achieved significance. Of the two, the Ecological Model explains greater variance. It, therefore, emerged as the most powerful predictor of out-of-home placements, of the models tested for this sample. Hypothesis 5 is supported by this analysis.

Hypothesis 6: An ecological set of variables including Age at Intake, Felony Offenses, use of a Ventilation coping strategy, and Number of Prior Placements, will better explain length of stay in the most recent placement, than will blocks that contain demographics, offense history, clinical characteristics, family characteristics, or placement history alone.

This hypothesis is intended to test the relative value of specified models as they compare to one another. They do not represent an exhaustive examination of alternative explanations for Length of Stay, but were built on specific rationales, as indicated below.

Each of the models specifies a group of variables that represent elements of the youth's social ecology. The demographic model, offense history model, clinical characteristics model, family characteristics model, and placement history model are each focused on a particular level of the social ecology. The ecological model selectively combines elements from each of these levels.

Age at Intake is included in the ecological model because placement data indicate that youth are typically placed at about 15 to 16 years old, and the juvenile justice laws at the time of these placements specified an endpoint for confinement at age 19. Release of serious felony offenders is subject to rigorous review by a State Board charged with protecting public safety, and the behavior of such offenders in placement would be likely to cause sanctions and longer periods of confinement. Use of a Ventilation coping strategy would appear to be more troublesome in a structured program, as it would serve to disrupt smooth agency operation and possibly antagonize staff members. Number of Prior Placements is used as an indicator of the youth's history in placement, and allows inclusion of this history without overlapping other variables and inducing a singularity problem.

Model 6 (Table 30) tests the relative value of demographics as they explain Length of Stay. It includes Age at Intake, Single Parent Family type, and Urban Environment. The demographic model explains about 6% of the variance (Adjusted R Square = .061), and shows significance (*p* .004). Within this model, Age at Intake is the best predictor of Length of Stay (*beta* -.274, *t*= -3.621, *p*= .000), while Single Parent Family (*beta* -.080, *t*= -1.057, *p*= .292) and Urban Environment (*beta* .094, *t*= 1.251, *p*= .213) do not make significant contributions.

Table 30: Demographic Regression Model for Length of Stay

R	R Square	Adjusted R Square	Standard Error
.278	.077	.061	6.297

	Sum of Squares	df	Mean Square	F	Signif
Regression	553.210	3	184.403	4.651	.004
Residual	6621.207	167	39.648		
Total	7174.418	170			

	Unstnd Beta	Stnd Error	Stnd Beta	t	Signif
Constant	41.365	7.410		5.582	.000
Age at Intake	-1.711	.472	-.274	-3.621	.000
Single Parent	-1.088	1.030	-.080	-1.057	.292
Urban Envir	1.543	1.233	.094	1.251	.213

Model 7 (Table 31) enters variables that represent offense history, including Status Offenses, Felony Offenses, and Adjudications. It explains about 3% of the variance (Adjusted R Square = .027), but does not achieve significance (*p*= .056). Only Felony Offenses adds explanation within this model (*beta* = -.185, *t*= -2.442, *p*= .016), while Adjudications (*beta* = -.046, *t*= -.605, *p*=.546), and Status Offenses (*beta* = -.109, *t*=-1.429, *p*=.155) have no appreciable explanatory value.

Table 31: Offense History Regression Model for Length of Stay

R	R Square	Adjusted R Square	Standard Error
.210	.044	.027	6.408

	Sum of Squares	df	Mean Square	F	Signif
Regression	316.676	3	105.559	2.571	.056
Residual	6857.741	167	41.064		
Total	7174.418	170			

	Unstnd Beta	Stnd Error	Stnd Beta	t	Signif
Constant	17.671	1.051		16.820	.000
Status Offs	-1.006	.704	-.109	-1.429	.155
Felony Offs	-.491	.201	-.185	-2.442	.016
Adjudications	-.134	.221	-.046	-.605	.546

Model 8 (Table 32) examines the contribution of clinical characteristics to an understanding of Length of Stay. It includes Family Tensions stressors, Personal Investment and Ventilation coping strategies, and Family Functioning. The model explains about 1% of the variance (Adjusted R Square = -.011), but is not significant ($p= .712$). Within the model, none of the individual independent variables emerge as valuable predictors of Length of Stay (Family Functioning *beta* = -.052, *t*= -.665, *p*= .507; Ventilation *beta* = .001, *t*= .014, *p*= .989; Personal Investment *beta* = .076, *t*= .959, *p*= .339; and Family Tensions *beta* = -.079, *t*= -.983, *p*= .327).

Table 32: Clinical Characteristics Regression Model for Length of Stay

R	R Square	Adjusted R Square	Standard Error
.112	.013	-.011	6.532

	Sum of Squares	df	Mean Square	F	Signif
Regression	90.786	4	22.697	.532	.712
Residual	7083.632	166	46.672		
Total	7174.418	170			

	Unstnd Beta	Stnd Error	Stnd Beta	*t*	Signif
Constant	16.294	4.121		3.953	.000
Fam Tensions	-.224	.248	-.079	-.983	.327
Prsnl Invstmt	.591	.616	.076	.959	.339
Ventilation	.009	.666	.001	.014	.989
Fam Functng	-.529	.797	-.052	-.665	.507

Model 9 (Table 33) utilizes family characteristics, including Single Parent Family Type, Family Tensions, and Family Functioning, as predictors of Length of Stay. Family Characteristics explain 1% of the variance in Length of Stay (Adjusted R Square = -.010, but the model is not significant (p= .711). In the structure of this model, neither independent variable is a good predictor of Length of Stay (Family Functioning *beta* = -.044, *t*= -.562, *p*= .575; Family Tensions *beta* = -.071, *t*= -.917, *p*= .360; and Single Parent Family *beta* = -.034, *t*= -.434, *p*= .665).

Table 33: Family Characteristics Regression Model for Length of Stay

R	R Square	Adjusted R Square	Standard Error
.090	.008	-.010	6.528

	Sum of Squares	*df*	Mean Square	F	Signif
Regression	58.679	3	19.560	.459	.711
Residual	7115.738	167	42.609		
Total	7174.418	170			

	Unstnd Beta	Stnd Error	Stnd Beta	*t*	Signif
Constant	18.200	2.859		6.365	.000
Single Parent	-.459	1.057	-.034	-.434	.665
Fam Tensions	-.217	.237	-.071	-.917	.360
Fam Functng	-.441	.788	-.044	-.562	.575

Model 10 (Table 34) applies placement history as a predictor of Length of Stay. It includes only Intake from Home, and Prior Placements as predictors. Model 10 explains less than one percent of the variance (Adjusted R Square = .006), and is insignificant (p= .221). In the context of this model, Prior Placements (*beta* = -.109, t= -1.425, p= .156) and Intake from Home (*beta* = .080, t= 1.047, p= .297) are not good predictors of Length of Stay.

Table 34: Placement History Regression Model for Length of Stay

R	R Square	Adjusted R Square	Standard Error
.134	.018	.006	6.476

	Sum of Squares	df	Mean Square	F	Signif
Regression	127.971	2	63.986	1.526	.221
Residual	7046.446	168	41.943		
Total	7174.418	170			

	Unstnd Beta	Stnd Error	Stnd Beta	t	Signif
Constant	15.002	1.209		12.407	.000
Intake Home	1.314	1.255	.080	1.047	.297
Prior Plcmnts	-.270	.190	-.109	-1.425	.156

Model 11 (Table 35) employs the ecological construction of variables described in the opening portion of this section. It uses Age at Intake, Family Functioning, Felony Offenses, and Prior Placements to explain Length of Stay. This model explains about 7 and-a-half percent of the variance (Adjusted R Square = .074), and is statistically significant (p= .002). Only Age at Intake achieves significance for its individual *beta* (-.230, t=-3.032, p= .003) within the model. Prior Placements (*beta* = -.113, t= -1.514, p= .132), Felony Offenses (*beta* = -.131, t= -1.715, p= .088), and Family Functioning (*beta* = -.050, t= -.660, p= .510) did not make individually significant contributions to this model.

Table 35: Ecological Regression Model for Length of Stay

R	R Square	Adjusted R Square	Standard Error
.309	.096	.074	6.252

	Sum of Squares	df	Mean Square	F	Signif
Regression	685.952	4	171.488	4.387	.002
Residual	6688.465	166	39.087		
Total	7174.418	170			

	Unstnd Beta	Stnd Error	Stnd Beta	t	Signif
Constant	40.902	7.669		5.334	.000
Age at Intake	-1.436	.474	-.230	-3.032	.003
Fam Functng	-.505	.764	-.050	-.660	.510
Felony Offs	-.347	.202	-.131	-1.715	.088
Prior Plcmnts	-.281	.186	-.113	-1.514	.132

Table 36: Summary of Regression Models for Length of Stay

Model	R	R Square	Adjusted R Square	Signif
Demographic	.278	.077	.061	.004
Offense History	.210	.044	.027	.056
Clinical Characteristics	.112	.013	-.011	.712
Family Characteristics	.090	.008	-.010	.711
Placement History	.134	.018	.006	.221
Ecological	.309	.096	.074	.006

The ecological model (Model 11) performs best in explaining Length of Stay when compared with the other five models in this analysis. It explains the highest percentage of variance and achieves statistical significance. This model performs better than the other models tested against it, and lends support to Hypothesis 6. Only the demographic model (Model 6) provides a worthwhile comparison, as the other four models performed poorly. The results of the models as explanations for Length of Stay are summarized in Table 36.

CHAPTER 7

Interpretations and Implications

This chapter highlights some of the significant findings of the study. The findings are integrated with each other and with prior knowledge using a topical approach, explanations and implications of the findings are presented, and additional suggestions for further research are offered. A final section considers the limitations and delimitations of the study.

MEASUREMENT ISSUES
This study supports the value of assessing the psychometrics of published measures when they are applied to under-researched populations. Structured investigation of social phenomena involves a fundamental decision about the relative value of normative research, which attempts to compare new knowledge to an established empirical base for purposes of generalization, and exploratory research, which works to increase available knowledge in an area that is not well-understood (Keppel & Zedeck, 1989).

Normative research that is focused on comparing samples with each other or to previously established standards, must utilize the same measures with each of those samples. To do otherwise would make direct comparisons impossible.

The utility of exploratory studies, however, may increase through application of particular measures that are specifically intended to elicit in-depth information about the sample under investigation (Jayaratne & Levy, 1979). Particular knowledge may be enhanced by measures that are optimized for the sample that is studied.

In this study, the clinical instruments used by the agency were carefully selected as measures of the variables that were addressed in the treatment program (Grasso and Epstein, 1987), and alternative minority ("non-White") norms were constructed for scoring the scales (Grasso, 1985). The purposes of these instruments were to assess therapeutic needs within a specified program and to evaluate program outcomes for diverse clients. Their use in normative research and program evaluation may be entirely appropriate.

As reflected in the results of the confirmatory factor analysis, however, this study found that a homogeneous population of African-American male delinquents lives with different constructions of stress, coping, and family functioning than do the samples with which these instruments were developed. Accurate measurement of these dimensions of life may require different constructs or scales than those used for the types of samples that are usually involved in instrument construction. Even when different cutting points or norms for a scale are established for different groups of people, conclusions about their behavior may be misinformed if the scales used to draw those conclusions are based on the patterns of a significantly different population. The inclusion of events in a stressor inventory, for example, beginning school or starting a new business, may not accurately measure contact with stressors if the sample in question lacks the economic resources to engage in such endeavors. In such a case, scales that cluster events related to poverty or limited opportunity may be more reflective of the actual experience of the participants. If a young man reports that his family did not experience the stress of someone starting a new job, that does not mean that the family did not experience stressors. Unless the range of items includes features of the social ecology of the group in question, serious distortions in conclusions are unavoidable.

This study highlights the crucial value of construct validity in such investigations. Psychometric assessment of existing scales provides the researcher with an opportunity to improve the construct validity of the measures, especially for the intended application. Such a step is also worthwhile in building a base of empirical findings. This approach is supported by the work of other researchers (Singleton, Straits, Straits, & McAllister 1988).

In addition to the need for acceptable reliability and construct validity, is the value of parsimony in applied research, especially with populations in restricted settings. In order to protect against exploitation of special populations, instruments that are short and understandable, easily administered, and relatively non-intrusive are desirable. The current study indicates that further development in the area of instrument construction would aid achievement of this value.

INTAKE CHARACTERISTICS OF THE SAMPLE
Demographic characteristics of the sample provided support for prior knowledge about delinquent samples. The average age of sample youth was close to that of national male delinquent samples generated by prior research (Sickmund 1998). The predominance of single parent families in the research sample fit earlier characterizations of delinquent samples (Whittaker, Tripodi, & Grasso, 1993). The finding that most of the sample youth came from urban environments is similarly without surprise (McCubbin, Kapp, & Thompson, 1993).

Offense, adjudication, and placement history data, however, raise important points for consideration. It is striking that 80% of these youth came into the most recent placement directly from their family homes. These youth may have been under some form of supervision, but were clearly not placed out of the home immediately prior to intake, despite a history of multiple serious offenses and prior placements. Their average of almost three felony offenses, with less than one status offense, would indicate that they should be considered to be high-risk candidates for recidivism. The fact that they averaged almost three adjudications and over two prior placements would also seem to indicate that previous attempts at control had not been effective. These findings raise questions about the criteria and process involved in placement decisions, and highlight an experience of repetitive placements that may only serve to perpetuate itself. Ashford and LeCroy (1993) offer a decision-making tree for placement decisions. Their protocol and similar guides would be useful targets for empirical testing as predictors of successful placement. If placement decisions are improved, it may be possible to break the cycle of multiple placements for African-American male delinquents.

Results regarding the experience of stressors and use of coping strategies provide information not previously available from other sources. These results indicate that sample youth are about evenly split in their preferences for prosocial coping behaviors as found in the personal investment factor, and the acting-out behaviors contained in the ventilation factor. Such results are, perhaps, counterintuitive when one thinks about the stereotypic juvenile delinquent, so additional investigation is warranted. It is possible that preferences for either coping strategy are the result of factors such as temperament, behavioral modeling, or exposure to particular life experiences. These variables are either unmeasured in the current study, or are only partially represented by the scales that were derived from the items of the published instruments. These findings cannot be readily compared to those for a similar sample, in part because of the decision to modify the published scales, but primarily due to the dearth of quantitative research on stress and coping of African-American male delinquents.

Family functioning of these youth was midrange on average, with little dispersion. As noted in Chapter 3, the vast body of research on delinquency indicates a significant incidence of low cohesion and low control in the families of delinquent youth (Sheilds & Clarke, 1995; Towberman, 1994; Vazroni & Flannery, 1997). Although there is no definitive reason to expect that characteristics common to families of delinquents are also determinants of out-of-home placement, these results should be approached with caution.

This study calls attention to the need to apply improved measures of family functioning variables to research with minority samples. The Family Functioning scale was constructed in the interest of improved psychometric properties. As described in Chapter 5, this was accomplished for this sample, but further improvement in validity may be necessary. This may occur through the application of scales that consist of different items. Measurement of family cohesion and parental control with increased sensitivity would probably yield more interpretable results.

In a study not bound by existing data, the selection of measures could consider instruments such as the McMaster Family Assessment Device (Epstein, Baldwin, & Bishop, 1983), or the Family Environment Scale (Moos & Moos, 1981). Both of these instruments contain specific subscales that measure cohesion and behavioral control. A worthwhile endeavor may be to factor-analyze the cohesion and control items from both of these instruments in order to specify a new combination for further testing with African-American samples. Regardless, instrument selection may be eased by consulting psychometric assessments of existing instruments, such as that conducted by Tutty (1995), who evaluated the relative strengths and weaknesses of several common family measures.

DELINQUENT BEHAVIOR AND OUT-OF-HOME PLACEMENT

Intuition implies that there is a linkage between delinquent behavior and subsequent out-of-home placements. The casual observer may even equate the two. Although such an assumption may appear logical on the surface, the results of this study emphasize a distinction between offenses and placements. Statistically significant correlations of Status Offenses, Felony Offenses, and Adjudications with Number of Out-of-Home Placements were not found. In fact, when Length of Stay in the most recent placement was considered as a representation of confinement, the number of Felony Offenses showed an inverse relationship.

These results suggest that a range of decision-making intervenes between delinquent activity and subsequent placement. The lack of observed correlations between adjudication and either status or felony offenses, let alone the placement variables, would also indicate that other factors influence the youth's formal journey through the juvenile justice system. Prior research has shown that about 67% of juvenile arrests find their way into juvenile court, and that only another 7% are referred directly to adult criminal court, while 25% of the cases end with police contact (Snyder, 1998). While these figures outline the proportion of disposition of cases, they do not elucidate the operative factors. Research targeted specifically at decision making within the juvenile justice system would help clarify these mechanisms.

Rather than concluding that delinquent behavior plays little to no role in impacting out-of-home placements, however, it is necessary to remember that the placement variables were constructed as accumulations, and that an additional range of mid-level misdemeanor offenses remains unmeasured in this study. Alternative measures of these variables may enhance understanding of the specific connections between offending behavior and confinement.

The observed inverse association of felony offenses with longer stays in placement raises additional empirical questions. One would expect that multiple felony offenders would be regarded by decision makers as more serious criminals than those with fewer offenses, and, thereby, incarcerated for relatively longer periods. The fact that this was not found in this study points to other explanations. Repeat felony offenders may be more sophisticated in manipulation, or possess greater motivation to gain release. It is also plausible that confinement could limit the opportunity to commit reported crimes, which could show itself as an inverse relationship between record of felonies and length of stay over more than one placement. Another possibility is that the African-American youth comprising this sample were subjected to more restrictive treatment than their European-American counterparts, in the form of detention and longer confinements, for less serious offenses, as noted in other research (Poe-Yamagata, 1997; Sickmund, Snyder & Poe-Yamagata, 1995).

EXPECTED ASSOCIATIONS WITH OUT-OF-HOME PLACEMENT

None of the variables that were expected to be associated with accumulation of out-of-home placements performed as expected. They include Age at Intake, Status Offenses, Felony Offenses, Adjudications, Family Tensions, and Ventilation.

These variables were selected for inclusion in the correlational hypothesis on the bases of prior research showing correlates of delinquency in general delinquent samples, and consistency with the clinical expectations of family oriented practitioners (Kelley, Loeber, Keenan, & DeLamatre, 1996; Krohn, Stern, Thornberry, & Jang, 1992; Nelson, 1990; Rankin & Wells, 1990, Sheilds & Clarke, 1995; Towberman, 1994). In addition, the Strain Theory and the Social Control Theory of delinquency contributed key variables to this analysis. Investigations of Strain Theory have shown that blockage from favored resources or interference with attempts to avoid unpleasant circumstances contribute to the formation of delinquent behavior (Elliot & Voss, 1974; Greenberg, 1977; Agnew, 1985). Tests of Social Control Theory have also substantiated its focus on effective structure and accountability in the context of emotional connections as mediators of delinquency (Bahr, 1979; Wells & Rankin, 1988). These theories contributed an emphasis on family, community, stress, and coping variables. The emphasis of Sub-Cultural Deviance Theory on negative peer associations (Briar & Piliavin, 1965; Short & Strodbeck, 1963) did not have available measures in these data. Similarly, there was no way to include the emphasis of Rational Choice Theory on economic forms of decision-making by the youth (Cornish & Clarke, 1986). Together, the included variables were intended to represent the social system characteristics of youth who were most likely to engage in delinquent acts, and who would be most in need of intervention. By focusing this analysis on placement, rather than delinquency, however, it has become apparent that established correlates and theories of delinquency may have limited utility in explaining out-of-home placement.

When focusing attention on the total accumulation of out-of-home placements, it is possible to consider the impact of program variables such as completion of treatment goals, and type of release from the program. In this study, completion of treatment goals was not correlated with the award of an approved release type. Of these two variables, only successful program completion is negatively associated with out-of-home placements. Therefore, practitioners may take heart in the fact that a focus on treatment goals may be more influential in limiting further out-of-home placements than administrative decisions regarding what kind of release the youth should be granted. The type of release granted does, however, show a meaningful association with a return to a home environment upon termination of the program placement, so it appears that youth who are seen as doing a good job in the program are more likely to be sent home upon release. No studies of similar variables are available with which to compare these findings. Thus, this study may open a new avenue of inquiry regarding planned release from the program, as well as placement options.

ADDITIONAL ASSOCIATIONS WITH OUT-OF-HOME PLACEMENT

The significant relationship of single parent family type with out-of-home placements was not specified in a research hypothesis, but was uncovered through correlational analysis. This finding is consistent with early research on families of delinquents, and more recent studies that focused on the relationship of family structure to delinquent behavior (Minuchin, Montalvo, Guerney, Rosman, & Schumer, 1967; McCubbin, Kapp, & Thompson 1993). Wells and Rankin (1991) state directly that children who live in homes with only one parent or in homes which have been disrupted by divorce or separation, are more likely to display a range of emotional and behavioral problems, including delinquency, than children from two-parent families.

Thornberry, Smith, Rivera, Huizinga, and Stouthamer-Loeber (1999) examined the effect of single parent family structure on youthful offenders with a probability sample of 4,000 families engaged in the Rochester, Denver, and Pittsburgh youth studies. They counted "family transitions" (which accounted for a change in family structure) over the course of the youth's involvement in the longitudinal study, and linked this variable to increased delinquent acts and illegal drug use. The researchers concluded that in Rochester and Denver, the number of family transitions had a clear and statistically significant effect on the prevalence of delinquency and drug use. While these results do not speak directly to the issue of out-of-home placement, they do highlight the preconditions for placement in the form of delinquent activity.

Benson and Roehlkepartain (1993) also found that being part of a single parent family was associated with increased risks for out-of-home placement. Identifying the specific conditions under which this is most likely is another challenge for future research.

Single parent family type may also exert indirect influence on the total accumulation of out-of-home placements as shown in the correlational schematic (Figure 5). It is represented as part of a link that connects prior placements, family functioning, and coping to aftercare placement at home. Other available research has not specifically validated this indirect influence, so replication of this study would be beneficial to build further understanding about such connections. On the basis of this study and prior research, however, it appears that being part of a single parent family is associated with being placed out of the home for African-American male delinquents.

Contrary to expectations, high family functioning was not shown to protect youth against accumulation of out-of-home placements. High family functioning was, instead, positively related to the number of prior placements. There is a possibility that temporary removal of the youth from the family home may help restore or induce some structural order to family functioning. The functions of family cohesion and parental control that surface so often in the delinquency treatment literature may be enhanced through external control. In addition, the proliferation of family intervention in delinquency treatment programs may also serve to enhance family functioning. These possibilities should not be construed as support for the necessity of long-term restrictive placements, however, as short-term respite arrangements or milder forms of external control such as diversion programs may be just as effective in this regard. Prior research that compares diversion and alternative control measures to traditional placement provides support for these approaches as effective interventions for reduction of delinquent behavior (Davidson, Redner, Blakely, Mitchell, & Emshoff, 1987; Northey, Primer, & Christensen, 1997).

Residence in an urban environment is not directly associated with out-of-home placement in the present study, but it may contribute to a chain of administrative decision making which affects release from placement, and return to a family home, thereby continuing the cycle of out-of-home placements. These linkages are depicted in Figure 5. It is likely that staff members in delinquency programs who make release decisions are less inclined to send a youth back to his home community if they believe that the community presents undue risks for recidivism. Indeed, the author has worked in settings where staff members made explicit statements about the futility of working with a young man for several months and then returning him to the same troubled neighborhood.

Roscoe and Morton (1994) found that the community in which the juvenile lives has a stronger effect on the likelihood of involvement in delinquency than do racial characteristics. It appears, however, that this conclusion was drawn without full consideration of the role of race in limiting housing decisions and other social resources that impact the location of residence. Where racism is operative, and segregated housing predominates, race and location of residence may overlap. It should also be noted that their research focuses on delinquent behavior, rather than out-of-home placement. Taken together, however, these findings suggest that being an African-American may influence the location of residence in a segregated setting, and that coming from an urban environment may contribute to delinquent behavior and the extension of out-of-home placements.

OTHER NOTABLE ASSOCIATIONS

The direct relationship of Ventilation to Aftercare Placement Home may be puzzling at first blush. One might expect that swearing and threatening people would be counterproductive in an effort to have residential staff members approve a return to one's family home. A plausible explanation, however, takes into account the fact that the ventilation data refer to the time of program intake. Perhaps the youth who demonstrates problems early in the program makes more observable progress in treatment than his more reserved peer, and thereby earns a release to his home environment. The results of this study, thus, provide information about the coping preferences of sample youth, and imply a connection between exposure of behavioral problems and eventual return home. The lack of specific results about coping factors in connection to out-of-home placement, however, should be regarded as inconclusive until work is conducted using more culturally relevant measures, and with other samples.

EXPLANATION OF MULTIPLE PLACEMENTS

A regression approach was used to explain the total accumulation of out-of-home placements. Models containing blocks of variables that represent demographics, offense history, clinical characteristics, and family characteristics, were compared with an ecological model that contained selected variables from each of the other blocks, as representations of subsystems of the youth's social ecology. The emergence of the ecological model as the only one with significance, as well as the highest explanatory value, indicates its relative value over the other models.

With the capacity of this analysis to isolate the unique contributions that separate variables within the block make to the explanation of variance, it is possible to uncover the value of variables that do not otherwise show significant or large correlations with the dependent variable (Tabachnick & Fidell, 1996). This is demonstrated in the ecological model, where single parent family type and family functioning share about equal value as the best individual predictors. The significance of the model that includes family characteristics is also notable. These results call additional attention to the potential value of developing measures of family functioning to improve prediction of out-of-home placement.

The performance of the ecological model in explaining multiple out-of-home placements may be further improved with the addition of decision-making variables. These could include the factors that are considered by delinquency services workers and agency intake workers when they decide to place a youth, such as assessment of community risk, open beds in residential placement, and assessment of the youth's family or neighborhood. Such a model would require a larger sample size, in order to gain enough statistical power to handle the number of included variables.

EXPLANATION OF DURATION OF PLACEMENT
A second set of regression models was used to explain duration of the most recent out-of-home placement. These models included variables in blocks to represent demographics, offense history, clinical characteristics, family characteristics, and placement history. They were compared with an ecological model that employed variables from each of these blocks to represent multiple levels of the youth's social ecology.

The ecological model outperformed the demographic model, which is the only other one to achieve statistical significance. The emergence of the demographic model as a good predictor of length of stay is noteworthy in that these characteristics are beyond the control either of the youth or the staff. Age at intake provides the greatest unique contribution in the model, and it is the least likely candidate for manipulation. The performance of the ecological model in explaining duration of placements, however, provides support for ecological theory as a framework for intervention. The greatest individual predictor in the ecological model is also age at intake. The similar performance of the age variable in both models would indicate that it might be usefully considered in an initiative to reduce disproportionate minority confinement through prevention programs. An approach that focuses on agency level placement decisions may also be useful in reducing length of stay.

DELIMITATIONS AND LIMITATIONS OF THE STUDY
This study focused exclusively on a homogeneous sample of African-American male delinquents. An integral part of the study was the decision to forego interesting comparisons by race, in order to obtain

more in-depth information about a group of youth that existing knowledge showed to be confined at comparatively higher rates than another group. For related reasons, a correlational design was chosen, and an existing dataset was employed. Each of these decisions established boundaries around the investigation. Much like an old wooden fence, this boundary serves to both protect the integrity of the findings about the sample, and to exclude opportunities for comparison.

Clearly, the limits of a naturalistic correlational design preclude generalization of these findings beyond the sample studied. Evidence also suggests that there may be some significant differences between the sample and the overall agency population in felony offense and adjudication history. Nonetheless, it is instructive to note that most of the youth placed at the host agency during the period of this data collection came through an intake and assessment committee comprised of staff members from several similar agencies. To qualify for inclusion in this pool, all youth had to be felony offenders, with similarly high scores on a community risk assessment tool. Assignment to a particular agency was then made primarily on the basis of program openings, so it may be that the sample youth have notable similarities to other agency populations. Replication of this study, using multiple measures and additional samples of African-American delinquents could address the research questions with greater rigor, thereby increasing the possibilities for generalization.

In addition to demonstrating the value of an ecological approach to understanding disproportionate minority confinement, this study has outlined additional work for the field. Valuable next steps in research may include better specification of clinical measures for African-American families, use of qualitative methods to obtain deeper understanding of the meanings of personal and family processes, application of an ecological approach with comparison groups, and extension of the ecological framework used here to include juvenile justice system factors that may be crucial elements of the problem. Specifically, information about formal and informal decision-making that impacts placement decisions would be very valuable. Interviews and ethnographic studies of decision making by staff who work in restrictive placements may also be useful in this regard.

IMPLICATIONS FOR FURTHER RESEARCH USING SYSTEMS DYNAMICS

In addition to the specific suggestions for further substantive investigation offered in the sections above, an alternative analytic method may be considered. In this study, the problem of disproportionate minority confinement was viewed as a systemic phenomenon. The findings of the study indicate that there is value in regarding out-of-home placement as the outgrowth of particular combinations of social ecology. While the correlational methodology used here yielded valuable results, clarity regarding relationships among such ecological variables could be greatly enhanced by applying a non-recursive approach. A non-recursive approach makes it possible to clearly represent reciprocal influence among variables, or what is called feedback, within the natural systems of the participants. In this way, it could be used to specify relationships among variables that represent various levels of the youth's social ecology.

A practical means of specifying and simulating the operation of such a non-recursive system is found in a computer-based orientation known as Systems Dynamics (Forrester, 1969). Appendix B describes this approach in more detail, but it is important to note that Systems Dynamics does a particularly good job of organizing one's thinking about specification of the complex mutual goal-seeking action of subsystems over time (Levine, Van Sell, & Rubin, 1992). Even if one is intimidated by the notion of constructing computer simulations, the process of identifying feedback in social systems can be very useful on a conceptual level.

Systems Dynamics has identified several common modes of operation for systems, which are referred to as basic flow processes (Cover, 1996) and are joined together as archetypes (Brierova, 1996). These archetypes describe the structure of the system and, based on the structure they specify, determine the behavioral output of the model.

Systems dynamicists often use diagrams to depict the movement of information or energy through a system (Cover, 1996). Initial pictures of the system use loop diagrams, and more advanced versions use flow diagrams that are run on a computer (Levine, Van Sell, & Rubin, 1992). Models are best conceptualized on the basis of existing theory and practical knowledge of the system, and the resulting models may be quantified with empirical data or estimates of the values of the parameters (Levine, 1992).

In order to advance understanding of disproportionate minority confinement, conceptual work on the feedback involved in the social ecology of African-American youth has been initiated and is offered here. Although the following description requires further specification in order to be used in an operating dynamic systems model, it may serve as a foundation for such an effort.

The problem of disproportionate minority confinement was approached, for purposes of this example, from the perspective of the Strain Theory of delinquency. As noted in the foregoing discussion, this theory is compatible with the analyses conducted in this study. It is also widely applied in the delinquency literature (Merton, 1938; Cloward & Ohlin, 1960; Agnew, 1992; McCluskey, 2002). Strain Theory emphasizes the importance of opportunity structures in the fulfillment of socially valued goals. The theory holds that a desire to participate in social structures and share in the fruits of affluent society that is blocked by environmental barriers, leads to formation of illegal attempts to gain wealth or social status (Agnew, 1985).

For purposes of Systems Dynamics modeling, it is possible to represent relevant constructs such as delinquency, out-of-home placement, and barriers to opportunity. Each of these constructs emerged as relevant to the study of disproportionate minority confinement.

The observed dynamics of disproportionate minority confinement may be captured by the system archetype known as "fixes that fail". This archetype has been outlined by Hannon and Mattias (1994). This structure may be represented in a loop diagram to depict the cycle of out-of-home placement for African-American males in the juvenile justice system.

The "fixes that fail" archetype recognizes that once a problem comes to light, a "fix" or perceived solution to that problem may be rapidly implemented (High Performance Systems, 1989). In this context, the solution brings about the immediate desired impact on the problem, which reduces its frequency or intensity. From a systemic perspective, this relationship of action to problem is conceptualized as a balancing loop or negative feedback loop (Levine, Van Sell, Rubin, 1992). Over time, however, an unintended consequence of the solution may be generated that actually exacerbates the original problem state (High Performance Systems, 1989). Systems analysts think of such an operation as a reinforcing loop or positive feedback loop (Levine, Van Sell, Rubin, 1992).

Figure 9: "Fixes that Fail" Loop Diagram

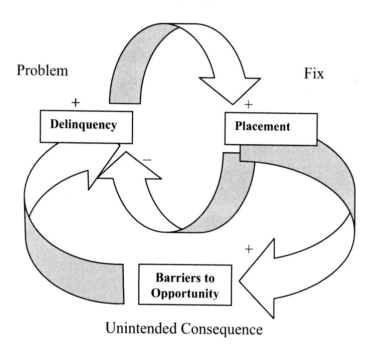

By applying the "fixes that fail" archetype to the problem of disproportionate minority confinement, it is possible to locate theoretical and practical systems variables within these loops. As may be seen in Figure 9, Delinquency is defined as the problem; Placement is instituted as the fix; and Barriers to Opportunity becomes the unintended consequence. Moving along the arrow that connects Delinquency to Placement, one may identify the beginning of the negative feedback loop that is intended to reduce the delinquent behavior of adolescents. For simplification, increases in Delinquency are shown to lead to increases in Placement by the positive arrow.

The immediate impact of Placement is a reduction in Delinquency as shown by the negative arrow from Placement to Delinquency. Such an attempt at solving the problem, however, may feed the need for continued or repeated placement as the use of that solution becomes compelling and necessary to contain the delinquency. This is depicted by the positive arrow from Delinquency to Placement, and a cycle of operation is identified.

The other loop in the diagram connects Placement with Barriers to Opportunity and then Delinquency. It represents the reinforcing or amplifying action of Placement on Delinquency through the unintended consequence of an increase in Barriers to Opportunity. By applying Strain Theory, one may hypothesize that barriers to socially accepted avenues of opportunity would generate additional delinquency. This may happen after a single stay in placement or be multiplied over the course of repeated cycles as indicated by the return arrow that connects Delinquency to Placement.

By embellishing this simple diagram, it is possible to add additional feedback structure. For example, one might identify additional consequences of placement, or other inputs to delinquency, such as undesirable peer relationships that echo throughout the system. This simple diagram may become very complex with such additions, so it is important for the analyst to start simply, add only required structure, and build a foundation for the model that is understandable but realistic (Levine, Van Sell, & Rubin, 1992).

Another means of representing this complexity is the flow diagram, a very simple example of which is found in Figure 10. Flow diagrams are used in computer programs that are designed to simulate the operations of complex dynamic systems. The flow diagram represents variables that accumulate as "stocks", and places them in boxes (Cover, 1996). Actions that add to or drain the accumulations are depicted as attendant "flows" (the objects with spigots that are attached to the stocks). These flows show the primary processes that fill or drain the stock variables. They are also one way of depicting the time it takes for stock variables to accumulate or dissipate. Inward flows have clouds attached to their leading edges to indicate that there is something outside the system. Similarly, outward flows have clouds attached to their trailing edges. Circles, called "auxiliaries", are used to represent several other necessary aspects of the system. These include algebraic and dimensional converters that are necessary for the mathematical computations completed by the computer program. Circles may also be used to represent other accumulating variables that are not of direct interest in the model. Arrows are used to connect the stocks to flows to indicate the impact of variables on each other.

Figure 10: Flow Diagram of Strain Theory Showing Effect of Placement

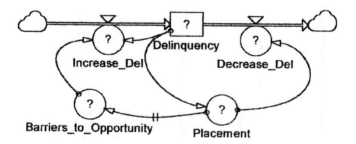

Figure 10, as noted, is a very simple flow diagram that is analogous to the loop diagram in Figure 9. It focuses on the delinquency sector of what could become a full model of disproportionate minority confinement, which would include several other ecological subsystems. Delinquency is represented as a stock, with Increase and Decrease in Delinquency shown as flows. Both Placement and Barriers to Opportunity are shown as circles for purposes of this simplistic presentation, but would be included as stocks with their own flows in a fully developed model.

In this diagram, the balancing loop is shown in the connection from Delinquency to Placement, and from Placement to Decrease in Delinquency. Because Decrease in Delinquency is the outflow of Delinquency, it is shown as the channel for reducing the frequency or severity of the problem. The feedback loop, which is shown by the arrows that connect each of these variables, indicates that this process is repetitive. This is the same process that is represented in the balancing loop of Figure 9.

In addition, Delinquency is thought to be driving its own production, as indicated by the feedback arrow to the inflow Increase. As delinquent thinking and acting accumulates, it is likely to continue to grow unless some intervention occurs. Another input to Increase in Delinquency is provided by Barriers to Opportunity. Barriers to Opportunity is, in turn, heightened over time by unsuccessful Placement. This is depicted by the arrow with hash marks that connects Placement to Barriers to Opportunity. The hash marks indicate a delay. The arrows that connect Placement to Barriers to Opportunity to Increase in Delinquency, and the feedback of Delinquency to its own Increase represent the reinforcing loop also shown in Figure 9.

Although these two figures are alternate methods of representing the same structure, the flow diagram may be used as a graphic interface for computer simulation of the system. The question marks inside the symbols of Figure 10 indicate that this model has not yet been quantified with data or estimates. In fact, it is far from ready for such quantification in its current state, as the structure must be verified and more detail must be introduced.

This brief description of the possibilities for application of dynamic systems modeling is meant to illuminate the value of conceptualizing and investigating disproportionate minority confinement as a problem that involves feedback in the social ecology of the African-American adolescent male. The reader is referred to Appendix B and its attendant references as resources for learning more about dynamic systems modeling.

IMPLICATIONS FOR JUVENILE JUSTICE POLICY

The present political polarization regarding incarceration and alternatives for delinquent youth has resulted in conflict on ideological and practical levels. Allocation of resources for incarceration and diversion has split the juvenile justice community. While control of criminal behavior is necessary to protect public safety, it is clear that the present form of confinement, which has been built on two-hundred years of practice, is not sufficient for either habilitating offenders or protecting society in the long term. The cycle of repeated removal from community and return home for participants in this study and nationally, indicates that an integrative approach might be worthy of consideration.

It would be possible to integrate social control with treatment intervention cooperatively rather than competitively through expansion of intensive community supervision programs that also provide culturally appropriate developmental experiences for young African-American men and boys. In conjunction with electronic or human supervision, educational and experiential programs that develop interpersonal and economic connections are likely to improve the chances that a young man will remain productive in his community.

The finding regarding the association of single parent families with an accumulation of out-of-home placements indicates that there is still a need for improved family policy initiatives. Resources for families should not just be economic, but interpersonal as well, because it is at the relational level that factors such as cohesion and internalized control are fostered. Specifically, increased opportunities to exchange social support in informal or formal networks should be expanded.

This study also calls attention to the decision-making processes used to determine who goes into placement and how long they stay. The overall discrepancy between proportions of African-American and European-American youth in placement is a compelling reason to examine the bases for decisions to confine youth. Such a reason is compounded, however, when one realizes that coming into a placement from home rather than another placement is more likely to lead to a return home than is the successful completion of a year-long treatment program. In the same regard, age plays a greater role in determining length of stay than does residence in an urban environment, or personal experience of stress and use of coping strategies. Indeed, a record of felony offenses matters less in accumulating out-of-home placements than does membership in a single parent family. Guidelines for placement decisions that equalize the risks and opportunities for African-American and European-American youth are greatly needed. At a minimum, these guidelines should include level of offense, clinical assessment of needs, and the community risk factors associated with their recidivism.

IMPLICATIONS FOR JUVENILE JUSTICE PRACTICE INTERVENTION

This study raises the value of prevention programs aimed at youth well below the age of 15, at which point the likelihood of placement reaches its peak. Older youth also accumulate a record of multiple offenses, even when they have been involved in more than one out-of-home placement. For these reasons, effective intervention programs should be developed to meet the needs of younger children, thereby providing alternatives to the experiences that produce delinquent behavior and subsequent out-of-home placement.

Findings that establish an inverse association between higher numbers of prior placements and longer lengths of stay call attention to the possibility that youth may not learn behaviors that keep them out of additional placements, but they do learn behaviors that help them get out of the next placement sooner. While this is not troubling by itself, it also appears that these same youth do not necessarily complete treatment goals, or earn favorable releases. Under these circumstances, it may be important to develop counterbalances to a practice effect by utilizing innovative treatment approaches or varied treatment settings.

The higher explanatory values of the ecological models for Number of Out-of-Home Placements and Length of Stay, indicate that intervention should be directed toward multiple levels of the youth's social ecology in order to decrease the incidence of minority placement. The current efforts of many agencies to include the family of the youth in intervention efforts could be expanded. Such expansion might focus on aspects of the youth's community, especially if that is an urban environment. A systemic approach would allow integration of efforts to improve functioning at multiple levels of the youth's social ecology.

CONCLUSION

This study applied an ecological framework to enhance understanding of the problem of disproportionate minority confinement. Particular analyses described the characteristics of a unique group of young men, examined the relationship of several factors at multiple levels of their social systems, and tested explanations for different forms of confinement. Results of the analyses further suggest that a systemic approach holds promise for explaining observed phenomena, identifying new areas for investigation, and developing innovative analytic tools for directed study, so that we might further our understanding of, and correct the occurrence of, disproportionate minority confinement.

Notes

CHAPTER ONE THROUGH CHAPTER SEVEN

CHAPTER 1

1. The 1988 amendments to the Juvenile Justice and Delinquency Prevention act (JJDP Act of 1974, Pub. L. No. 93-415, 42 U.S.C. 5601 et seq.) specified the responsibilities of states participating in the Formula Grants Program. These states must determine whether disproportionate confinement of the specified minority populations exists, and demonstrate efforts to reduce it. States are required to "address efforts to reduce the proportion of juveniles detained or confined in secure detention facilities, secure correctional facilities, jails, and lockups who are members of minority groups if such proportion exceeds the proportion such groups represent in the general population."

2. Professional ethics in the helping professions require that even involuntary recipients of service be afforded opportunities to make decisions that affect their lives within the limits of legal sanctions. See Hepworth, Rooney, & Larsen (2001), and Corey, Corey, & Callanan (2003).

CHAPTER 2

1. The most recent meta-analysis discussed here (Pope, Lovell, & Hsia, 2002) searched the target literature using terms such as "disproportionate minority confinement", "juvenile justice processing", and "juvenile justice and African-Americans". The search sought

information regarding the primary racial and ethnic groups specified in federal legislation, as well as gender-specific findings. Searches were conducted in the Criminal Justice Abstracts, the Sociological Abstracts, Social Science Citation Index, and the Legal Resource Index.

2. The second meta-analysis highlights the increased methodological precision in more recent studies of racial effects in the juvenile justice system. The precision of newer studies has allowed a focus on other variables of potential importance, as well as refinement of the reasons why disproportionality occurs (Pope, Lovell, & Hsia, 2002).

3. Finding more "mixed effects" in later studies does not mean that disproportionality is decreasing. Pope, Lovell, & Hsia (2002) point out that disproportionality differs at the various stages juvenile justice processing, and that the legally relevant variables which are often studied (offense history, current charge, etc.) may not be the source of disproportionality.

CHAPTER 3

1. The graphic depicting the arrangement of social control and social treatment is included to help the reader visualize a symmetrical linkage of the two forces. It is not intended to be a literal representation of the time-line of developments in juvenile justice.

2. *Parens Patriae* is Latin for "parent of his country". It has been used to refer to a doctrine that positions the state as the guardian of children. Under this doctrine, the state is supposed to act as a benevolent parent on behalf of a child (Ferdinand, 1991; Hatchett, 1998).

3. The quotations from Carpenter (1969) were originally published in 1851.

4. The presentation of modern practice approaches is included as an overview of current forms of out-of-home placement, as well as alternatives to out-of-home placement. These options are all readily available to decision-makers in juvenile justice and have been empirically validated to varying degrees.

5. Several forms of family therapy have been used with families of delinquents. Now "traditional" forms include Structural Family Therapy and Strategic Family Therapy, but newer models such as

Functional Family Therapy (Alexander & Parsons, 1982) have also been used to good effect with adolescents.

6. Electronic tethers have been used as an alternative to secure detention for relatively low-risk property offenders. These tethers involve the attachment of a metal band to the wrist or ankle of an individual youth, which must be inserted into a device on a telephone, in response to random phone calls from the supervising agency. In this way, there is a means of controlling the physical whereabouts of the youth, without literal incarceration. (During the initial proposal for use of these devices in Michigan, the author participated in meetings where many agency administrators objected to their use. One African-American executive was especially troubled by the similarity to what he referred to as "the chains of slavery".)

7. The analytic techniques that are referred to as "survival analysis" or "event history analysis" recognize that an offender is not likely to re-offend while in a secure placement. In order to accurately assess the recidivism rates, therefore, it is necessary to account for the length of time that the offender is "exposed" to the community. These techniques provide statistical control for the length of time to recidivate (Benda, Toombs, & Peacock, 2002; Kapp, Schwartz, & Epstein, 1994).

CHAPTER 4

1. Bronfrenbrenner's (1979) ecological model is particularly well-suited to the study of African-American male juvenile delinquents. It may be applied to focus attention on the youth's transactions with his environment, including peer relationships, family patterns, school experience, gang activity, economic opportunity, employment, classism, racism, and public policy initiative. This framework views such factors as interdependent elements of an open system.

2. Although Millgram (1989) defines "coping" as positive adaptations to stressors, the term is used more broadly in this study to encompass all types of attempts to mediate stressful situations. Such a definition is consistent with the measurement instruments used for data collection.

3. An alternative to Millgram's (1989) model, known as the Resiliency Model of Family Adjustment and Adaptation, has been advanced by McCubbin, Thompson, & McCubbin (1996). This

comprehensive model evolved from earlier conceptualizations. It asserts that families achieve long term adaptation through a process of adjustment that involves the degree of family vulnerability based on the "pile up" of stressors and family type, the family's assessment of the impact of the stressors, and available coping resources.

4. For more information on family assessment instruments and their measurement characteristics, the reader is referred to Fredman and Sherman (1987), Jordan and Franklin (1995), and Gehring, Debry, and Smith (2001).

CHAPTER 5

1. The concept of "incremental validity" applies to the contribution of this study. Sechrest (1963) coined the term to describe the value of exploratory work in a previously uninvestigated or under-researched field. Incremental validity holds that learning more about a phenomenon than was previously known provides inherent value for those engaged in that area.

2. The clinical information system that was developed and maintained at the agency, has been described by Grasso and Epstein (1987). At the time of data collection, it integrated several clinical assessment instruments, case tracking data, and management and supervision information.

3. Data were collected at intake and release from the program for each youth. There were no repeated measures of clinical characteristics utilized, as the focus of this study was not on changes produced by a treatment effect. Variables such as completion of treatment goals, type of release, and length of stay were used to capture movement through the youth's respective program.

4. High confidence in procedures used to collect data on clinical characteristics is warranted. The instruments were each standardized and lent themselves to patterned administration. Although consistency of administration of these clinical assessment instruments was not assessed directly (there was no opportunity to compute inter-rater reliability), uniformity of procedures was protected by training and monitoring conducted by a fully staffed program evaluation department within the agency. In addition, all clinical staff who administered the assessment instruments were trained and supervised by dedicated

clinical supervisors who were thoroughly versed in collection and application of the data (Mooradian & Grasso, 1993).

5. Informed consent procedures were regimented, documented, and carefully observed by agency administrators. Signed release forms were collected for each case.

6. The sample size of 171 cases is adequate for the analyses conducted. Adequacy of the sample size was assessed following the procedure specified by Tabachnick and Fidell (1996). With an interest in both overall models and individual variable effects, it was determined that a sample size of 110 cases would support up to six independent variables in standard multiple regression, with significance set at .05, and an expected effect size of .15. With 171 cases, a margin of safety is observed for smaller observed effect sizes, distribution problems, or measurement error.

7. Distributions of the placement and ecological variables were analyzed for kurtosis and skewness and, where appropriate, were transformed to improve the analyses, as recommended by Tabachnick and Fidell (1996). These variables include Out-of-Home Placements, Number of Placements, Prior Placements, Total Out-of-Home Placements, Adjudications, Length of Stay, Age at Intake, Status Offenses, Felony Offenses, Family Tensions, Personal Investment, Ventilation, and Family Functioning.

8. The design used in this study may be considered to be a naturalistic or observational design, in that naturally occurring events are the object of investigation, and the experiences of the participants are not subject to experimental manipulation. The study may also be termed exploratory in its attempt to better understand a social problem about which little is known. The design suits the explanatory intent of the investigation.

9. Confirmatory Factor Analysis is used to check the psychometric properties of previously established scales (Hunter & Hamiliton, 1992).

10. The original subscales of the A-FILE, regardless of modification, would not pass the test for parallelism when they were tested against each other. Parallelism is a concept that allows a statistical test of the distinctiveness of each group of items from all other tested groups of items. Some variations of these scales, however, passed the significance test for internal consistency, which indicates the degree to which the items within the scale are alike one another.

During the analysis, it appeared that the items in the A-FILE might be unidimensional, that is, that they might express only one scale. Even as a single scale, however, it was not possible to pass the test for parallelism when these items were included in a factor analysis with the coping and family functioning items of the ACOPE and the FACES II. These results indicated that taken together, the items used to measure stressors by the A-FILE could not be distinguished from those used to measure coping by the ACOPE, or family functioning measured by the FACES II for this sample. The development of a new "leaner" scale was chosen to address this problem.

11. The original distributions of the placement variables evidenced problems with kurtosis and skewness and were transformed using a natural log transformation following directives offered by Tabachnick and Fidell (1996). For descriptive and regression analyses, the observed distributions of *Prior Placements* and *Number of* Placements were used for consistency of interpretation. For the correlations and correlational schematic, transformed *Adjudications, Prior Placements,* and *Total Out-of-Home Placements* were employed in order to improve the analysis.

12. The *Length of Stay* variable showed a normal distribution and was not transformed for any of the analyses.

13. To measure the *Single Parent Family* variable, the original codes from the Intake Data Form were recoded as follows: Code 0=1 Reconstituted, 2 Nuclear, 4 Foster, 5 Adoptive, 6 Extended. Code 1=Single Parent.

14. It is recognized that the *Urban Environment* variable holds a place as a proxy for what could be a more advanced measure of the youth's environment. Wayne, Oakland, and Macomb counties were included as the recognized "tri-county" metropolitan area of the city of Detroit; Saginaw county was included because of its inclusion of the city of Saginaw; and Genessee county was included because it contains the city of Flint. All other counties were coded as Not Urban. This coding scheme was uncomplicated by sample youth coming from counties with marginal urban areas, and a relatively high degree of confidence in its ability to represent urban environments is thereby imparted.

15. To measure the original codes from the Intake Data Form were recoded as follows: Code 0=3 Group Home, 5 Jail, 6 Youth Home, 7

Shelter, 8 Private Care Facility, 9 State Institution, 10 Mental Hospital, 11 Other. Code 1=Family as described in Family Type, 2 Family other than as described in Family Type, 4 Independent Living.

16. To measure *Successful Program Completion*, the original codes of the Intake Data Form were recoded as follows: Code 0=3 Some, 4 None, 5 Not Applicable. Code 1=1 All, 2 Most.

17. To measure *Successful Release*, the original codes of the Intake Data Form were recoded as follows: Code 0=3 Administrative Discharge, 4 Administrative Termination, 5 Court Termination, 6 State Termination, 7 Inactive (extended truancy). Code 1=1 Agency Release, 2 Administrative Release.

18. To measure *Aftercare Home Placement,* the original codes from the Intake Data Form were recoded as follows: Code 0=3 Foster Care, 5 Private Residential, 6 Group Home, 7 County Residential, 8 Psychiatric Institution, 9 State Institution, 12 Non-Secure Shelter, 13 Other, 14 Unknown (usually used for youth who are truant from the authorized placement). Code 1= 1 Parent's Home, 2 Relative's Home, 4 Adoptive Home, 10 Independent Living, 11 Armed Services.

19. Standard Multiple Regression Analysis was deemed more appropriate for the present analysis than hierarchical or stepwise procedures due to the lack of empirical knowledge about the relationships of the independent and dependent variables. Standard Multiple Regression is more consistent with the exploratory nature of the study.

CHAPTER 6

1. When testing the psychometrics of the published clinical assessment instruments, the CFA program in Package was used (Hunter & Hamiliton, 1992). In this program, significance of the internal consistency chi square tests for deviation from a unidimensional within-cluster correlation matrix that allows for a variation in item quality. This means that it is assumed that the items within a factor form a single dimension with items that make different levels of contribution to the factor (they have different correlations with the underlying factor, or factor loadings). The Chi Square test allows assessment of significance of difference from the single dimension. A

significant difference means that the item is not a good contributor to the measurement of the factor.

2. Internal consistency is assessed on the basis of item-factor correlations. Significance of the parallelism Chi Square tests for parallel with allowance for variation in item quality (Hunter & Hamilton, 1992). Parallelism refers to a form of external consistency of a scale. If items of a scale measure the same construct, then their pattern of relationships to items outside the scale should be similar, or parallel. This pattern is assessed with ratios of scale items to items from other included scales to determine their distinctiveness from one another.

3. For the frequency analysis that addresses Research Question 1, categorical rather than dichotomous forms of the variables, and untransformed distributions of the continuous variables, were used to simplify interpretation.

4. For purposes of the correlation and regression analyses, the recoded version of the family type variable, in the form of Single Parent Family Type is used instead of the categorical levels of the variable.

5. For comparison of the study sample to the agency population on the characteristics of age at intake, adjudications, status offenses, felony offenses, and the number of previous placements, the means of the sample were compared with the means of the population using a one-sample t-test. Agency population values were used as the test values, a two-tailed test was computed, and a 95% confidence interval was constructed.

6. For all comparisons between the study sample and the agency population, 95% confidence intervals were also constructed as a way to provide information beyond the significance of differences found with the t test. The confidence interval for age at intake shows that in 95 of 100 cases the difference would be nearly non-significant (l=-.529, u=-.214).

7. The t test used for felony offenses was conducted with equal variances not assumed due to the results of Levene's Test, F=77.995, p= .000). The t test showed the difference to be statistically significant (p=.000). Even using a 95% confidence interval (l=1.17, u=1.91), the difference remains significant.

8. The difference between the study sample and the agency population in number of adjudications indicated by the *t* test remains significant using a 95% confidence interval ($l=.31$, $u=.97$).

9. The correlation matrix in Chapter 6 presents the observed values. Appendix A presents the values for these correlations corrected for attenuation (Hunter & Hamilton, 1992). This procedure shows what the correlations would be without the effect of measurement error. It is based on a formula that divides the observed correlation by the product of the square roots of the reliabilities of the variables.

10. The reader is reminded that use of a one-tailed test for significance of a correlation is appropriate when the valence (negative or positive) of the correlation is specified. Likewise, the use of a two-tailed test is appropriate when an association is tested, but the valence is not specified.

11. Although the schematics in Chapter 6 resemble causal models, the reader is cautioned not to interpret them as such. Path analysis was not attempted because the models were constructed post-hoc, which would be a violation of accepted rules for specification of causal models (Asher 1983). Here, interest is focused only on observed relationships among the variables. While extensive quantitative analysis of path models is possible, the interest of this study requires only that the linkage effects are interpreted. The interested reader will be able to compute the path coefficients for direct and indirect effects, relative values of compound paths, and the effect of residuals, from the correlation matrix shown in Table 23, using formulae suggested by authors such as Asher (1983).

In each of the diagrams, Aftercare Placement Home is treated separately from Total Out-of-Home Placements for purposes of clarity, although placement in a family setting would mean that no additional out-of-home placement would be added to the prior and agency placements. No direct connection from Prior Placements to Total Out-of-Home Placements is shown. This linkage was omitted in the model because the computation of Total Out-of-Home Placements includes Prior Placements. The correlation is, therefore, meaningless due to lack of singularity.

In order to construct meaningful diagrams, connections among variables which are located in the same column required decisions about directionality of the linkages. While this is clearly incompatible with a purely correlational approach (which only locates associations without identifying directionality of the linkages), the purpose of this diagram is to move toward a better informed causal understanding. With this goal in mind, the rationales for the linkages as shown are offered here.

Age at Intake is negatively correlated with Single Parent Family type as another exogenous variable. At the exogenous, or initial, level of the model, bi-directional arrows are used to show that no direction of influence may be imparted. In other words, these two variables co-exist in time, and logic alone is not sufficient to assign an order to them.

The clinical characteristics also show effects among themselves. Order is assigned based on two assumptions. It is assumed that Family Functioning shapes the Personal Investment coping strategies available to the youth through child rearing and relational experiences. It is also assumed that the stressor, Family Tensions, affects the use of Ventilation coping strategies because coping strategies are defined as responses to stressful situations. Because Personal Investment coping strategies are linked directly with Family Functioning, Personal Investment is used as an input to Ventilation, rather than ordering the association in the opposite direction. These orderings of the associations are generally supported by theory in the form of the Resiliency Model of Family Stress, Adjustment, and Adaptation (McCubbin & McCubbin, 1991).

The program level variables also exhibit associations that may be viewed as mutual influence. At this level, however, the decision was made to establish Length of Stay as the input to Successful Release, because there is an accumulation of time, and presumably effort during that time, that produces the award of an approved release from the program. Certainly, agency knowledge indicates that youth who are immediately released from the programs are not able to "earn" their release. Those who stay an exceptionally long time, however, may also be released for other reasons.

12. Multiple Regression Model 1 shows no problem with autocorrelation of residuals as indicated by a Durbin-Watson statistic of 1.801 (*l* 1.693, *u* 1.774, $p = .05$). The Durbin-Watson statistic indicates no concern with autocorrelation when the value is near 2.

Autocorrelation of residuals would confound interpretation of the multiple regression model.

13. There is no conclusive reason for concern about the correlation of residuals within Multiple Regression Model 2 (Durbin-Watson = 1.755, *l* 1.679, *u* 1.788, *p*= .05).

14. For Regression Model 3, correlation of residuals presents no significant risk with a Durbin-Watson statistic of 1.806 (*l* 1.679, *u* 1.788, *p*=.05).

15. The Durbin-Watson statistic for Multiple Regression Model 4 is acceptable at 1.835 (*l* 1.693, *u* 1.774, *p* .05).

16. The Durbin-Watson statistic for Regression Model 5 is 1.791, which indicates no significant problem with correlation of adjacent residuals (*l* 1.679, *u* 1.788, *p*.05).

17. For Regression Model 6, the Durbin-Watson statistic, at 1.213, shows problems with autocorrelation of residuals (*l* 1.693, *u* 1.774, *p* .05). A decision was made not to correct for this problem, because all models compared in this section of the analysis evidence similar values. This is not considered a problem for interpretation of these results because the focus is only on comparison of the models with each other, not for purposes of generalization to other samples, or to uncover the best possible model of all alternatives.

18. For Regression Model 7, the Durbin-Watson value is 1.271 (*l* 1.693, *u* 1.744, *p*= .05). This indicates a problem with autocorrelation of residuals in the model. It was treated in the same way as Model 6.

19. The Durbin-Watson statistic for Regression Model 8 has a value of 1.201 (*l* 1.679, *u* 1.788, *p* .05), which indicates a problem with autocorrelation of residuals. It was treated similarly to Model 6 and Model 7.

20. For Regression Model 9, the Durbin-Watson value is 1.173 (*l* 1.693, *u* 1.774, *p* .05), which indicates a problem with autocorrelation of residuals. This model was treated in the same way as Model 6, Model 7, and Model 8.

21. Regression Model 10 has a Durbin-Watson value of 1.183 (*l* 1.706, *u* 1.760, *p* .05) which indicates a problem with autocorrelation of residuals. It was treated in the same manner as Model 6, Model 7, Model 8, and Model 9.

22. The Durbin-Watson statistic for Model 11 is 1.261 (*l* 1.679, *u* 1.788, *p* .05), which indicates a problem with autocorrelation of

residuals. It was treated in the same manner as Model 6, Model 7, Model 8, Model 9, and Model 10.

CHAPTER 7

1. The regression models were constructed *a priori*, on the basis of research and practice knowledge, and were not influenced by the correlations which were obtained later.

2. Due to the standard regression method used in this study, it is inappropriate to compare the relative explanatory value of individual variables outside the context of their own block. These characteristics of the individual variables represent the unique contribution that they make within that set of variables and should not be confused with the beta values that would result from stepwise regression methods.

3. Because archetypes can streamline the construction of a running systems dynamics model, cautions have been raised about the risks of model misspecification that are inherent in misapplying an archetype for the sake of simplicity (Brierova, 1996).

Correlation Matrix Showing Correction for Attenuation

This appendix contains Table 37, which presents the corrrelations among study variables as corrected for attenuation. This procedure applies a formula wherein the observed correlation is divided by the product of the square roots of the reliabilities of the correlated variables.

It represents a method of showing what the correlations would be without the effect of measurement error. A comparison of Table 23 (observed correlations) with Table 37 (correlations corrected for attenuation) allows the reader to discern the effect of measurement error on the associations. The only correlations that display changes from Table 23 to Table 37 are those that involve variables drawn from the clinical measures. These variables were derived from scales obtained by questionnaires and have computed reliabilities. All other variables were reported directly as counts, and are, therefore, assumed to have perfect reliabilities.

Table 37: Correlation Matrix of Ecological Variables Corrected for Attenuation (part one)

	Age	Single Parent	Urban	Home Intake	Status	Felony	Adjudication	Prior Placement	Family Tensions
Age									
Single Parent	-.15*								
Urban	.11	.08							
Home Intake	.05	-.04	.061						
Status	-.10	.10	-.07	.14					
Felony	.23*	.08	.00	.08	-.09				
Adjudication	-.02	-.06	.04	-.15*	-.09	.01			
Prior Placement	-.06	.16*	-.03	.01	-.02	-.02	.05		
Family Tensions	.07	.02	.09	-.03	.00	.05	.05	-.03	

* significant at *p*<.05   ** significant at *p*<.01

Table 37: Correlation Matrix of Ecological Variables Corrected for Attenuation (part two)

	Age	Single Parent	Urban	Home Intake	Status	Felony	Adjudication	Prior Placement	Family Tensions
Personal Investment	.04	-.11	.03	.15	-.05	-.04	-.04	.03	.16
Ventilation	.09	.00	.05	.06	-.04	-.06	.04	.01	-.38**
Family Functioning	-.05	-.11	.00	-.04	-.03	-.12	-.01	.18*	.07
LOS	-.25**	-.03	.06	.08	-.09	-.18*	-.02	-.17*	-.09
Successful Goals	.03	.08	-.01	-.04	-.02	.06	-.04	-.18*	.11
Successful Release	-.07	-.05	-.20*	-.05	-.15	-.10	.05	-.04	-.11
Aftercare Home	.09	-.12	.14	.17*	-.12	-.06	-.06	-.01	-.18*
Number of Placements	-.06	.16*	-.03	.01	-.02	-.02	.05	x	.09
Total Placements	-.08	.20*	-.06	-.06	-.02	.00	.06	x	.13

* significant at $p<.05$ ** significant at $p<.01$

x Total Placements is computed by adding 1 to Number of Placements, so a correlation is meaningless.

Table 37: Correlation Matrix of Ecological Variables Corrected for Attenuation (part three)

	Personal Investment	Ventilation	Family Function	LOS	Success Goals	Success Release	Aftercare Home	# Plcmnts	Total Plcmnts
Personal Investment									
Ventilation	-.26**								
Family Function	.22*	-.14							
LOS	.07	.02	-.05	-.02					
Success Goals	-.15	.09	-.03						
Success Release	-.06	.12	-.12	.46**	-.04				
Aftercare Home	.05	.20*	.09	.19*	-.02	.33**			
# Plcmnts	.03	.01	.18*	-.17*	-.18*	-.04	-.01		
Total Plcmnts	.04	-.04	.15	-.20*	-.15*	-.11	-.28**	x	

* significant at *p*<.05   ** significant at *p*<.01

x Total Placements is computed by adding 1 to Number Placements, so a correlation is meaningless.

Systems Dynamics

Systems dynamics grew out of general systems theory and cybernetics. It was invented in the late 1950's by Jay Forrester at MIT (Forrester, 1969; Cover, 1996). He was among the first to develop a method of representing complex human systems in mathematical and computer-based terms. The original tenets of systems dynamics have survived a translation into more accessible applications that may be run on personal computers. Systems dynamics stands as a causal approach to utilizing time-series data. It is a means of representing networks of dynamic feedback structures that may be applied with an heuristic or empirical approach (Levine, Van Sell, & Rubin, 1992). These feedback structures are based on positive feedback loops which amplify behaviors, and negative feedback loops which reduce or restore levels of behaviors. Combinations of positive and negative feedback loops in the same system serve to produce variations in behavior over time.

Although it requires careful attention to model building, the systems dynamics approach allows considerable advantage over correlational techniques through its ability to handle mutual causality among variables. In this way, it is superior to path analysis, and provides an effective means of modeling non-recursive causal structures. There is a considerable body of knowledge regarding generic structures and patterns of system behavior to inform the construction of models (Hannon & Mathias, 1994; Breierova, 1996).

Dynamic system models are represented by flow diagrams that depict the relationships among variables. These diagrams include Stocks (variables that accumulate or dissipate over time such as "inventory"), Flows (action variables that lead to the accumulation or dissipation of the stocks such as "production" or "shipments"), Auxiliaries (variables that are used to algebraically combine other components of the system such as "desired inventory"), Constants (the parts of the system that do not change over the course of the analysis such as "workforce"), and Arrows (the connections among variables that indicate the direction of influences on each other). Once a diagram is produced, the variables are quantified, either with empirical data or estimated values, and the system is "run" on the computer to determine its behavior. This output appears graphically, over a selected time period, and is compared to the known behavior of the system to assess the accuracy of the structure represented in the diagram. It is possible to test the behavior of the system by using extreme values for the parameters of the system. After the model's behavior adequately matches what is known about the observed system, then it is possible to proceed with simulations of various intervention approaches to uncover their impacts on the system at various points in time and to inform decision making.

The systems dynamics approach is particularly well-suited to understanding many cyclical problems due to its ability to deal with several interacting variables over time and allow simulation of changes in the system. Systems dynamics seeks the explicit or implicit goals of the system in an attempt to identify conflicting sets of structure and other difficulties associated with a particular problem. It also characteristically incorporates cybernetic feedback among variables in order to follow the flow of information and energy through the system and realistically reflect causal structures. Lags in perception and delays in decision-making can be represented as a means of incorporating the time involved in systemic processes and understanding the differential effects of the same type of action at alternative points in time. Non-linear, as well as linear relationships among variables are recognized, to more accurately reflect impacts on each other. In short, systems dynamics views the action of systems in process rather than event terms, and recalls the analogy of the movie in comparison to the snapshot.

Even in investigations where full time-series data are not available for all relevant variables, a heuristic model may be constructed and quantified with a combination of observed and estimated values, to capture the qualitative behavior of the system (Levine, 1992). The model may then be used to test various interventions in subsequent simulations.

References

Additon, H.S., Deardorff, N.R. (1919). That child. *The Survey*, 33(April-Sept),185.

Agnew, R. (1985). A revised strain theory of delinquency. *Social Forces*, 64,151-167.

Agnew, R. (1992). Foundation for a general strain theory of crime and delinquency. *Criminology*, 30, 47-87.

Alexander, J., & Parsons, B. (1982). *Functional family therapy.* Monterey, CA: Brooks Cole.

Aneshensel, C.S., Rutter, C.M., Lachenbruch, P.A. (1991). Social structure, stress, and mental health: competing conceptual models. *American Sociological Review*, 56(April),166-178.

Asher, H.B. (1983). *Causal Modeling.* Newbury Park, CA: Sage.

Ashford, J.B. (1988). Protecting the interests of juveniles on aftercare/parole. *Children and Youth Services Review*, 18(7), 637-654.

Austin, J., Leonard, K.K., Pope, C.E., & Feyerhem, W.H. (1995). Racial disparities in the confinement of juveniles: Effects of crime and community social structure on the punishment. In K.K. Leonard, C.E. Pope, & W. Feyerhelm (Eds.) *Minorities in Juvenile Justice.* Thousand Oaks, CA: Sage.

Bahr, S. (1979). Family determinants and effects of deviance. In Burr, W., Hill, R., Nye, F.I., & I. Reiss, (Eds.), *Contemporary theories about the family*. New York: Free Press.

Barth, R.P. (1989). Theories guiding home-based intensive family preservation services. In Kinney, J., Haapala, D., & C. Booth. (Eds.), *Keeping families together: the homebuilders model*. (pp. 91-113). Hawthorne, NY: Aldine de Gruyter.

Barton, C., & Alexander, J.F. (1981). Functional family therapy. In Gurman, A.S.& D.P. Kniskern (Eds.), *Handbook of family therapy*. New York: Brunner Mazel.

Barton, W.H., & Butts, J.A. (1990). Viable options: intensive supervision programs for juvenile delinquents. *Crime and Delinquency*. 36(2), 238-256.

Bazemore, G., & Umbreit, M. (2001). *A comparison of four restorative conferencing models*. Washington, DC: U.S. Department of Justice, Office of Justice Programs, Office of Juvenile Justice and Delinquency Prevention.

Beavers, R. (1985). *Manual of beavers-timberlawn family evaluation scale and family style evaluation*. Dallas, TX: Southwest Family Institute.

Bednar, R.L., Burlingame, G.M., & K.S. Masters, (1988). Systems of family treatment: substance or semantics. *Annual Review of Psychology*, 34, 401-434.

Benda, B., Toombs, N.J., Peacock, M. (2002). Ecological factors in recidivism: A survival analysis of boot camp graduates after three years. *Journal of Offender Rehabilitation*, 35(1), 63-85.

Benson, P.L., & Roehlkepartain, E.C. (1993). Single-parent families. *Search Institute Source*, 11(2), 1-3.

Bilchuk, S. (1998). A juvenile justice system for the 21st century. *Crime and Delinquency*, 44(1), 89-101.

Briar, S., Piliavin, I. (1965). Delinquency, situational inducements and commitment to conformity. *Social Problems*, 13, 35-45.

Bridges, G.S., Conley, D.J., Engen, R.L., & Price-Spratlen, T. (1995). The role of race in juvenile justice in Pennsylvania. In K.K. Leonard, C.E. Pope, & W. Feyerhelm (Eds.) *Minorities in Juvenile Justice.* Thousand Oaks, CA: Sage.

Bridges, G.S. & Steen, S. (1998). Racial disparities in official assessments of juvenile offenders: Attributional stereotypes as mediating mechanisms. *American Sociological Review* 63(4), 554-570.

Brierova, L. (1996). Mistakes and misunderstandings: use of generic structures and reality of stocks and flows. *Massachusetts Institute of Technology. Systems Dynamics in Education Project.*

Brinson, J.A. (1994). The incarceration of black males: unsettled questions. *Journal of Offender Rehabilitation*, 20(3-4), 85-95.

Bourduin, C.M. (1995). Multi-systemic treatment of serious juvenile offenders: Long-term prevention of criminality and violence. *Journal of Consulting and Clinical Psychology*, 63(4), 569-578.

Bronfrenbrenner, U. (1979). *The ecology of human development: Experiments by nature and design.* Cambridge, MA: Harvard University.

Bruno, F. (1957). *Trends in social work 1874-1956: A history based on the proceedings of the national conference on charities and corrections.* New York: Columbia University Press.

Burton, D., Foy, D.W., Bwanausi, C., & J. Johnson, (1994). The relationship between traumatic exposure, family dysfunction, and post traumatic stress symptoms in male juvenile delinquents. *Journal of Traumatic Stress*, 7(1), 83-93.

Butler, K. (1997). The anatomy of resilience. *The Family Therapy Networker*, March/April, 22-31.

Butts, J.A., & Mitchell, O. (2000). *Criminal Justice 2000, Volume 2.* Washington, DC: U.S. Department of Justice, Office of Justice Programs, Office of Juvenile Justice and Delinquency Prevention.

Carpenter, M. (1969). *Reformatory schools for the children of the perishing and dangerous classes and for juvenile offenders.* New York: Kelly.

Chamberlain, P., & Rosicky, J.G. (1995). The effectiveness of family therapy in the treatment of adolescents with conduct disorders and delinquency. *Journal of Marital and Family Therapy*, 21(4), 441-459.

Cloward, R.A., Ohlin, L.E. (1960). *Delinquency and opportunity.* New York: Free Press.

Coffeen, E.L. (1910). National conference on the education of backward, truant, and delinquent children. *The Survey*, 24(April-Sept), 488.

Cohen, A. (1955). *Delinquent boys.* New York: Free Press.

Colon, F. (1981). Family ties and child placement. In Sinanoglu, P.A. & A.N. Maluccio, (Eds.), *Parents of children in placement: perspectives and programs.* New York: Child Welfare League of America.

Constantine, L.L. (1986). *Family paradigms: the practice of theory in family therapy.* New York: The Guilford Press.

Corey, G., Corey, M.S., Callanan, P. (2003). *Issues and ethics in the helping professions.* Pacific Grove, CA: Brooks/Cole.

Cornish, D.B., & Clarke, R.V. (1986). *The reasoning criminal: rational-choice perspectives on offending.* New York: Springer-Verlag.

Coughlin, D.D., Maloney, D.M., Baron, R.L., Dahir, J., Daly, D.L., Daly, P.B., Fixsen, D.L., Phillips, E.L., & Thomas, D.L. (1982). Implementing the community-based teaching family model at boys town. Boys Town.

Cover, J. (1996). *Introduction to systems dynamics* . Reston, VA: Powersim Press.

Cousins, L. (1997). Toward a socio-cultural context for understanding violence and disruption in black urban schools and communities. *Journal of Sociology and Social Welfare*, 24(2), 41-63.

Cronin, R.C. (1994). *Boot camps for adult offenders and juvenile offenders: Overview and update*. National Institute of Justice Research in Brief. Washington, DC: U.S. Department of Justice, National Institute of Justice.

Davidson, W.S., Redner, R., Blakely, C.H., Mitchell, C.M., & Emshoff, J.G. (1987). Diversion of juvenile offenders: an experimental comparison. *Journal of Consulting and Clinical Psychology*, 55(1), 68-75.

de Anda, D., Javidi, M., Jefford, S., Komorowski, R., & Yanez, R. (1991). Stress and coping in adolescence: a comparative study of pregnant adolescents and substance abusing adolescents. *Children and Youth Services Review*, 13, 171-182.

Decomo, R.E. (1998). Estimating the prevalence of juvenile custody by race and gender. *Crime and Delinquency* 44(4), 289-506.

Dembo, R., Dudell, G., Livingston, S., Schmeidler, J. (2001). Family empowerment as an intervention strategy in juvenile delinquency. *Journal of Offender Rehabilitation* 33(1), 1-32.

Dembo, R., Ramirez-Garcia, G., Schmeidler, J., Rollie, M, Livingston, S., Hartsfield, A. (2001). Long term impact of a family empowerment intervention on juvenile offender recidivism. *Journal of Offender Rehabilitation* 33(1), 33-58.

Deutsch, L.J. (1989). Early life events as discriminators of socialized and undersocialized delinquents. *Journal of Abnormal Child Psychology*, 17(5), 541-551.

Eamon, M.K. (1994). Institutionalizing children and adolescents in private psychiatric hospitals. *Social Work*, 39(5), 588-594.

Elliott, D., & Voss, H. (1974). *Delinquency and dropout*. Lexington, MA: Lexington Books.

Ellwood, C.A. (1910). The instability of the family as a cause of child dependence and delinquency. *The Survey*, 23(April-Sept), 889.

Empey, L. (1982). *American delinquency: its meaning and construction*. Homewood, IL: Dorsey.

Epstein, N., & Bishop, S. (1983). The mcmaster family assessment device. *Journal of Marital and Family Therapy*, 9, 171-180.

Eron, L., Walder, L., & Lefkowitz, M. (1971). *Learning of aggression in children*. Boston, MA: Little, Brown.

Feld, B.C. (1995). Policing juveniles: Is there bias against youth of color? In K.K. Leonard, C.E. Pope, & W. Feyerhelm (Eds.) *Minorities in Juvenile Justice*. Thousand Oaks, CA: Sage.

Ferdinand, T.N. (1991). History overtakes the juvenile justice system. *Crime and Delinquency*, 37(2), 204-224.

Frazier, C.E., & Bishop, D.M. (1995). The DMC initiative: The convergence of policy and research themes. In K.K. Leonard, C.E. Pope, & W. Feyerhelm (Eds.) *Minorities in Juvenile Justice*. Thousand Oaks, CA: Sage.

Fredman, N., & Sherman, R. (1987). *Handbook of measurements for marriage and family therapy*. New York: Brunner-Mazel.

Forrester, J.W. (1969). *Urban dynamics.* Portland, OR. Productivity Press.

Gehring, T.M., Debry, M., Smith, P.K. (2001). *The family system test (FAST): Theory and application.* Philadelphia: Brunner-Routledge.

Germain, C.B., & Bloom, M. (1999). *Human behavior in the social environment: An ecological view.* New York: Columbia University.

Gibbs, J.T. (1989). Black adolescents and youth: An update on an endangered species. In R.J. Jones (Ed.) *Black adolescents.* (pp. 3-28). Berkeley, CA: Cobb & Henry.

Grasso, A.J. (1985). *Boysville research manual.* Clinton, MI. Boysville of Michigan.

Green, R.G., & Vosler, N.R. (1992). Issues in the assessment of family practice: An empirical study. *Journal of Social Service Research,* 15(3-4), 1-19.

Greenberg, D. (1977). Delinquency and the age structure of society. *Contemporary Crises* 1, 66-86.

Goldberg, D., & Hodes, M. (1992). The poison of racism and the self-poisoning of adolescents. *Journal of Family Therapy,* 14, 51-67.

Gorman-Smith, D., Tolan, P.H., Zelli, A., & Huesmann, L.R. (1996). The relation of family functioning to violence among inner-city youths. *Journal of Family Psychology,* 10(2), 115-129.

Gray-Ray, P., & Ray, M.C. (1990). Juvenile delinquency in the black community. *Youth & Society,* 22, 67-84.

Grasso, A.J., Epstein, I., & Tripodi, T. (1988). Agency-based research utilization in a residential childcare setting. *Administration in Social Work,* 12, 61-80.

Hatchett, G. (1998). Why we can't wait: the juvenile court in the new millennium. *Crime and Delinquency*, 44(1), 83-88.

Henggeler, S.W. (1997). Treating serious anti-social behavior in youth: The MST approach. *Juvenile Justice Bulletin*. Washington, DC: U.S. Department of Justice, Office of Justice Programs, Office of Juvenile Justice and Delinquency Prevention.

Henggler, S.W., Melton, G.B., & Smith. L.A. (1992). Family preservation using multi-systemic treatment: an effective alternative to incarcerating serious juvenile offenders. *Journal of Consulting and Clinical Psychology*, 60(6), 953-961.

Hepworth, D.H., Rooney, R.H., Larsen, J. (2002). *Direct social work practice: Theory and skills.* Pacific Grove, CA: Brooks/Cole.

High Performance Systems (1989). *Manual for Stella II.* Hanover, N.H. High Performance Systems, Inc.

Hoffman, J.P., & Su, S.S. (1997). The conditional effects of stress on delinquency and drug use: a strain theory assessment of sex differences. *Journal of Research in Crime and Delinquency*, 34(1), 46-78.

Howell, J.C. (1998). NCCD's survey of juvenile detention and correctional facilities. *Crime and Delinquency.* 44(1), 102-109.

Hsia, H. M., & Hamparian, D. (1998). Disproportionate minority confinement: 1997 update. *Juvenile Justice Bulletin.* September 1988. Washington, D.C.: U.S. Department of Justice, Office of Justice Programs, Office of Juvenile Justice and Delinquency Prevention.

Hunter, J.E., & Hamilton, M.A. (1992). *Manual CFA.BAS -- A program in basica to do confirmatory factor analysis.* East Lansing, MI. Michigan State University.

Jayaratne, S., & Levy, R.L. (1979). *Empirical clinical practice.* New York: Columbia University Press.

Johnson, J.B., & Secret, P.E. (1990). Race and juvenile court decision making revisited. *Criminal Justice Policy Review* 4(2), 159-187.

Johnson, R.E., Marcos, A.C., & Bohr, S. (1987). The role of peers in the complex etiology of adolescent drug use. *Criminology*, 25, 323-340.

Johnson, W.W. (1996). Transcarceration and social control policy: the 1980's and beyond. *Crime and Delinquency*, 42(1), 114-124.

Jordan, C., & Franklin, C. (1995). *Clinical assessment for social workers: Quantitative and qualitative methods*. Chicago: Lyceum.

Kantor, D., & Lehr, W. (1990). *Inside the family*. San Francisco, CA: Jossey-Bass.

Kapp, S.A., Schwartz, I.M., & Epstein, I. (1994). Adult imprisonment of males released from residential childcare: a longitudinal study. *Residential Treatment for Children and Youth*, 12(2), 19-36.

Kelley, B.T., Loeber, R., Keenan, K., & DeLamatre, M. (1997). Developmental pathways in boys' disruptive behavior. *Juvenile Justice Bulletin*. Washington, DC: U.S. Department of Justice, Office of Justice Programs, Office of Juvenile Justice and Delinquency Prevention.

Keppel, G., & Zedeck, S. (1989). *Data analysis for research designs: analysis of variance and multiple regression/correlation Approaches*. New York: W.H. Freeman & Co.

Kilsdonk, A.G. (1983). *Human ecology: Meaning and usage*. East Lansing, MI: College of Human Ecology.

King, A.E.O. (1997). Understanding violence among young african-american males: an afrocentric perspective. *Journal of Black Studies*, 28(1), 79-96.

Kinney, J., Haapala, D., Booth, C., & Leavitt, S. (1989). The homebuilders model. In Kinney, J., Haapala, D. & C. Booth (Eds.), *Keeping families together: the homebuilders model.* (pp. 37-67). Hawthorne, N.Y: Aldine de Gruyter.

Krohn, M.D., Stern, S.B., Thornberry, T.P., & Jang, S.J. (1992). The measurement of family process variables: the effect of adolescent and parent perceptions of family life on delinquent behavior. *Journal of Quantitative Criminology,* 8(3), 287-315.

Krona, D. (1980). Parents as treatment partners in residential care. *Child Welfare,* 59, 91-96.

Lab, S.P., & Whitehead, J.T. (1988). An analysis of juvenile correctional treatment. *Crime and Delinquency,* 34(1), 60-83.

Lane, W.D. (1915). At the bar of childhood. *The Survey,* 35(October 1915-March 1916): 570.

Lattimore, F.L. (1910). Childrens' institutions and the accident problem. *The Survey,* 24(April-Sept), 801.

Leiber, M.J., & Jamieson, K.M. (1995). Race and decision making within juvenile justice: The importance of context. *Journal of Quantitative Criminology* 11(4), 363-388.

Leiby, J. (1978). *A history of social welfare and social work in the united states.* New York: Columbia University Press.

Len, M., (1988). Parental discipline and criminal deviance. *Marriage and Family Review,* 12(1-2): 103-112.

Levine, R.L. (1992). An introduction to qualitative dynamics. In Levine, R.L. & H. Fitzgerald (Eds.), *Analysis of Dynamic Psychological Systems Volume 1.* (pp. 267-330). New York. Plenum Press.

Levine, R.L., Van Sell, M., Rubin, B., (1992). System dynamics and the analysis of feedback processes in social science and behavioral systems. In Levine, R.L. & H. Fitzgerald (Eds.), *Analysis of Dynamic Psychological Systems Volume 1*. (pp. 145-266). New York. Plenum Press.

Loeber, R., Wung, P., Keenan, K, Giroux, B., Stouthammer-Loeber, M., Van Kammen, W., & Maughan, B. (1993). Developmental pathways in disruptive child behavior. *Development and Psychology*, 5, 103-133.

Maluccio, A., & Fein, E. (2002). Family preservation in perspective. *Family Preservation Journal* 6(1), 1-7.

Mauer, M. & Huling, T. (1995). *Young black men and the criminal justice system: Five years later.* Washington, DC: The Sentencing Project.

McCluskey, C.P. (2002). *Understanding Latino Delinquency: The Applicability of Strain Theory by Ethnicity.* New York: LFB Scholarly.

McConkey-Radetzki, N. (1987). The development of a family therapy program within a residential treatment setting: phases, issues, and strategies. *Journal of Strategic and Systemic Therapies*, 6, 16-28.

McCubbin, H.I., Fleming, W.M., Thompson, A.I., Neitman, P., Elver, K., Savas, S.A. (1995). Resiliency and coping in "at-risk" African-american youth and their families. In H.I. McCubbin, E.A. Thompson, A.I. Thompson, & J.A. Futrell (Eds.) *Resiliency in ethnic minority families: African-American families Volume 2.* Madison, WI: University of Wisconsin.

McCubbin, H.I., Kapp, S.A, & Thompson, A.I. (1993). Monitoring family system functioning, family and adolescent coping in the context of residential treatment: implications for program management, practice innovation, and research. In Grasso, A.J. & I. Epstein (Eds.), *Information systems in child, youth, and family agencies: planning, implementation, and service enhancement.* (pp. 155-174). New York: Haworth.

McCubbin, M.A., & McCubbin, H.I. (1991). Family stress theory and assessment: the resiliency model of family stress, adjustment, and adaptation. In McCubbin, H.I. & J.M. Patterson (Eds.), *Family assessment inventories for research and practice.* (pp. 3-34). Madison, WI: University of Wisconsin.

McCubbin, M.A., & McCubbin, H.I. (1996). Resiliency in families: A conceptual model of family adjustment and adaptation in response to stress and crises. In H.I. McCubbin, A.I. Thompson, & M.A. McCubbin (Eds.) *Family assessment: Resiliency, coping, adaptation – Inventories for research and practice.* (pp. 1-64). Madison, WI: University of Wisconsin.

McCubbin, H.I., & Patterson, J.M. (1991). ACOPE: adolescent-coping orientation for problem experiences. In McCubbin, H.I. & J.M. Patterson (Eds.), *Family assessment inventories for research and practice.* (pp. 235-254). Madison, WI: University of Wisconsin.

McCubbin, H.I., & Patterson, J.M. (1991). A-FILE: adolescent-family inventory of life events and changes. In McCubbin, H.I. & J.M. Patterson (Eds.) *Family assessment inventories for research and practice.* (pp. 101-112). Madison, WI: University of Wisconsin.

McCubbin, H.I., Patterson, J.M, Bauman, E., & Harris, L.H. (1981). Adolescent - Family Inventory of Life Events and Changes, *Family inventories.* St. Paul, MN: Family Social Science.

McCubbin, H.I., Thompson, A.I., Elver, K. (1995). Family attachment and changeability index (FACI8). In H.I. McCubbin, A.I. Thompson, & M.A. McCubbin (1996). *Family assessment: Resiliency, coping, and adaptation inventories for research and practice.* (pp. 725-752). Madison: University of Wisconsin.

McCubbin, H.I., Thompson, A.I., McCubbin, M.A. (1996). *Family assessment: Resiliency, coping, and adaptation inventories for research and practice.* Madison, WI: University of Wisconsin.

McGaha, J., & Fournier, D.G. (1988). Juvenile justice and the family: a systems approach to family assessment. *Deviance and the Family.* New York: Haworth.

McGarrell, E.F. (1993). Trends in racial disproportionality in juvenile court processing: 1985-1989. (Special Issue: reinventing juvenile justice - research directions) *Crime and Delinquency,* 39(1), 29-48.

McGarrell, E.F. (2001). Restorative justice conferences as an early response to young offenders. *Juvenile Justice Bulletin.* Washington, DC: U.S. Department of Justice, Office of Justice Programs, Office of Juvenile Justice and Delinquency Prevention.

Merton, R. (1938). Social structure and anomie. *American Sociological Review,* 3, 672-682.

Meyers, L.J. (1992). Transpersonal psychology: The role of the afrocentric paradigm. In A.K.H. Burlew, W.C. Banks, H.P. McAdoo, & D.A. ya Azibo (Eds.) *African-american psychology.* (pp. 5-18). Newbury Park: Sage.

Millgram, N.A. (1989). Children under stress. In Chadwick, T.H. & M. Herson (Eds.), *Handbook of child psychopathology.* New York: Plenum.

Minuchin, S., Montalvo, B., Guerney, B.G., Rosman, B.L., & Schumer, F. (1967). *Families of the slums: an exploration of their structure and treatment.* New York: Basic Books.

Montgomery, J.B. (1909*). Proceedings of the conference on the care of dependent children held at washington d.c.. january 25, 26, 1909.* Washington, D.C.: Government Printing Office.

Moon, M.M., Sundt, J.L., Cullen, F.T., Wright, J.P. (2000). Is child saving dead? Public support for juvenile rehabilitation. *Crime and Delinquency* 46(1), 38-60.

Mooradian, J., & Grasso, A.J. (1993). The use of an agency-based information system in structural family therapy treatment. *Child and Youth Service,* 16(1), 49-74.

Moos, R.H., & Moos, B.S. (1981). *Family environment scale manual.* Palo Alto, CA: Consulting Psychologists Press.

Nelson, K. (1990). Family-based services for juvenile offenders. *Children and Youth Services*, 12, 193-212.

Nichols, M.P., & Schwartz, R.C. (2001). *Family therapy: Concepts and methods.* Needham Heights, MA: Allyn and Bacon.

Northey, W.F., Primer, V., Christensen, M.S. (1997). Promoting justice in the delivery of services to juvenile delinquents: the ecosystemic natural wrap-around model. *Child and Adolescent Social Work Journal*, 14, 1, 5-22.

Nye, F.I. (1958). *Family relationships and delinquent behavior.* New York: John Wiley.

Office of Children and Youth Services (1988). *Families first guidelines.* Lansing, MI: Michigan Department of Social Services.

Olson, D.H., Portner, J., & Bell, R. (1982). FACES II: Family adaptability and cohesion evaluation scales. In D.H. Olson, H.I., McCubbin, H. Barnes, A. Larsen, A., M. Muxen, & M. Wilson (Eds.), *Family inventories.* (pp. 5-24). St. Paul, MN: Family Social Science, University of Minnesota.

Olson, D.H., McCubbin, H.I., Barnes, H., Larsen, A Muxen, M., & Wilson, M. (1982). *Family inventories: Inventories 'sed in a national survey of families across the life cycle.* St. Paul: Uni ersity of Minnesota.

Olson, D.H., Tiesel, J. (1991). *FACES II: linear sco. ng & interpretation.* St. Paul, MN. Family Social Science University of Minnesota.
Oppat, S. (1998). New maxey director focuses on i provement. *Ann Arbor News.* July 5, 1998. B-1, B-3.

Patterson, G.R. (1983). Stress: a change agent for fa ily process. In Garmezy, N., & M. Rutter (Eds.), *Stress, coping, and development in children.* New York: McGraw-Hill.

Pearlin, L.I. (1989). The sociological study of stress. *Journal of Health and Social Behavior,* 30, 241-256.

Perosa, L.M, & Perosa, S.L. (1990). The use of biploar item format for FACES III: A reconsideration. *Journal of Marital and Family Therapy,* 16(2), 187-199.

Peters, M., Thomas, D., & Zamberlan, C. (1997). Boot camps for juvenile offenders. Washington, DC: U.S. Department of Justice, Office of Justice Programs, Office of Juvenile Justice and Delinquency Prevention.

Petrosino, A., Turpin-Petrosino, C., & Finckenauer, J.O. (2000). Well meaning programs can have harmful effects! Lessons from experiments such as Scared Straight. *Crime and Delinquency* 46(3), 354-379.

Pierce, B.K. (1869). *A half century with delinquents or the new york house of refuge and its times.* New York: D. Appleton & Co.

Platt, (1977). *The child savers: The invention of delinquency.* Chicago, IL: Chicago Press.

Pope, C.E., & Feyerherm, W. (1990). Minority status and juvenile justice processing. *Criminal Justice Abstracts*, 22(2), 327-336; 527-542.

Pope, C.E., Lovell, R., & Hsia, H. (2002). Disproportionate minority confinement: A review of the research literature from 1989 through 2001. *Juvenile Justice Bulletin*. Washington, DC: U.S. Department of Justice, Office of Justice Programs, Office of Juvenile Justice and Delinquency Prevention.

Pumphrey, R., & Pumphrey, M. (1961). *The heritage of American social work*. New York: Columbia University Press.

Rankin, J.H., & Wells, L.E. (1990). The effect of parental attachments and direct controls on delinquency. *Journal of Research on Crime and Delinquency*. 27(2), 140-165.

Robbins, M.S., & Szapocznik, J. (2000). Brief strategic family therapy. *Juvenile Justice Bulletin*. Washington, DC: U.S. Department of Justice, Office of Justice Programs, Office of Juvenile Justice and Delinquency Prevention.

Rosella, J.D. (1993). Toward an understanding of the health status of black adolescents: an application of the stress-coping framework. *Issues in Comprehensive Pediatric Nursing*. 16(4), 193-205.

Russell, C.B., & Rigby, L.M. (1906). *The making of the criminal*. New York: MacMillan and Co.

Samuels, S.K., & Sikorsky, S. (1990). *Clinical Evaluations of School-Aged Children: A Structured Approach to the Diagnosis of Child and Adolescent Mental Disorders*. Sarasota, FL. Professional Resource Exchange.

Schiele, J.H. (1997). An afrocentric perspective on social welfare philosophy and policy. *Journal of Sociology and Social Welfare*, 24(2), 21-39.

Sechrest, L. (1963). Incremental validity: A recommendation. *Educational and psychological measurement.* 23(1), 153-158.

Shadish, W.R., Montgomery, L.M., Wilson, P, Wilson, M.R., Bright, I., & Okwumabua, T. (1988). Effects of family and marital psychotherapies: a meta-analysis. *Journal of Consulting and Clinical Psychology,* 61, 992-1002.

Shields, G., & Clark, R.D. (1995). Family correlates of delinquency: cohesion and adaptability. *Journal of Sociology and Social Welfare.* 22(2), 93-106.

Short, J.F. , & Strodbeck, F.L. (1963). The response of gang leaders to status threats: An observation on group process and delinquent behavior. *American Journal of Sociology,* 68(5), 571-579.

Sickmund, M., Snyder, H.N., & Poe-Yamagata, E. (1995). Juvenile offenders and victims: a national report. *Juvenile Justice Bulletin.* Washington, D.C.: United States Department of Justice Office of Juvenile Justice and Delinquency Prevention.

Sickmund, M., Snyder, H.N., & Poe-Yamagata, E. (1997). Juvenile offenders and victims: 1997 update on violence. *Juvenile Justice Bulletin.* Washington, D.C.: U.S. Department of Justice, Office of Justice Programs, Office of Juvenile Justice and Delinquency Prevention.

Snyder, H.N. (1998). Juvenile arrests 1997. *Juvenile Justice Bulletin.* Washington, D.C.: U.S. Department of Justice, Office of Justice Programs, Office of Juvenile Justice and Delinquency Prevention.

Snyder, H.N. (1999). Minorities in the juvenile justice system. *Juvenile Justice Bulletin.* Washington, D.C.: U.S. Department of Justice, Office of Justice Programs, Office of Juvenile Justice and Delinquency Prevention.

Spaccarelli, S. (1997). Psychological correlates of male sexual aggression in a chronic delinquent sample. *Criminal Justice and Behavior*, 24(1), 71-95.

Steiner, H., Garcia, I.G., & Matthews, Z. (1997). Post traumatic stress disorder in incarcerated juvenile delinquents. *Journal of the American Academy of Child and Adolescent Psychiatry*, 36(3), 357-359.

Stern, M., & Zevon, M.A. (1990). Stress, coping, and family environment: the adolescent's response to naturally occurring stressors. *Journal of Adolescent Research*, 5(3), 290-305.

Stiffman, A.R., Dore, P., & Cunningham, R.M. (1996). Violent behavior in adolescents and young adults: a person and environment model. *Journal of Child and Family Studies*. 5(4), 487-501.

Stinchcomb, J.B., & Terry, W.C. (2001). Predicting the likelihood of rearrest among shock incarceration graduates: moving from beyond another nail in the boot camp coffin. *Crime and Delinquency* 47(2), 221-242.

Sutphen, R.D., Thyer, B.A., & Kurtz, D.P. (1995). Multisystemic treatment for high-risk juvenile offenders. *International Journal of Offender Therapy and Comparative Criminology*, 39(4), 327-334.

Sutton, J.R. (1988). *Stubborn Children*. Berkeley, CA: University of California Press.

Tabachnick, B.G., & Fidell, L.S. (1996). *Using Multivariate Statistics* New York: HarperCollins

Tate, D.C., Reppucci, N., Dickon, B., & Mulvey, E.P. (1995). Violent juvenile delinquents: treatment effectiveness and implication for future action. *American Psychologist*, 50(9), 777-781.

Taylor, C.S. (1990). *Dangerous Society*. East Lansing, MI: Michigan State University.

Thornberry, T.P., Smith, C.A., Rivera, C., Huizinga, D., & Stouthammer-Loeber, M. (1999). Family disruption and delinquency. *Juvenile Justice Bulletin*. Washington, DC: U.S. Department of Justice, Office of Justice Programs, Office of Juvenile Justice and Delinquency Prevention.

Towberman, D.B. (1994). Psychosocial antecedents of chronic delinquency. *Young Victims, Young Offenders*, 151-164. *Juvenile Justice Bulletin*. Washington, DC: U.S. Department of Justice, Office of Justice Programs, Office of Juvenile Justice and Delinquency Prevention.

Turner, J.R., Wheaton, B., & Lloyd, D.A. (1995). The epidemiology of social stress. *American Sociological Review*, 60(April), 104-125.

Tutty, L.M. (1995). Theoretical and practical issues in selecting a measure of family functioning. *Research on Social Work Practice*, 5, 1, 80-106.

Vaux, A., & Ruggiero, M. (1983). Stressful life change and delinquent behavior. *American Journal of Community Psychology*, 11(2), 169-183.

Vazronyi, A., & Flannery, D.J. (1997). Early adolescent delinquent behaviors: association with family and school domains. *Journal of Early Adolescence*, 17(3), 271-293.

Weiss, H.B. (1990). Beyond *parens patriae*: building policies and programs to care for our own and others' children. *Children and Youth Services Review*, 12, 269:284.

Wells, L.E., & Rankin, J.H. (1988). Direct parental controls and delinquency. *Criminology*, 26, 256-285.

Wells, L.E., & Rankin, J.H. (1991). Families and delinquency: A meta-analysis of the impact of broken homes. *Social Problems* 38(1), 71-83.

Wenz-Gross, M., Siperstein, G.N., Untch, A.S., & Widaman, K.F. (1997). Stress, social support, and adjustment of adolescents in middle school. *Journal of Early Adolescence*, 17(2), 129-151.

Whittaker, J.K. (1979). *Caring for troubled children*. San Francisco, CA: Jossey-Bass.

Whittaker, J.K., Tripodi, T., Grasso, A.J. (1993). Youth and family characteristics, treatment histories, and service outcomes: some preliminary findings from the boysville research program. In A.J. Grasso & I. Epstein (Eds.), *Information systems in child, youth, and family agencies:planning, implementation, and service enhancement*. (pp. 139-154). New York: Haworth.

Whittaker, J.K. (2002). The elegant simplicity of family preservation practice: Legacies and lessons. *Family Preservation Journal* 6(1), 9-29.

Wolfgang, M.E., Figlio, R.M., & Sellin, T. (1972). *Delinquency in a birth cohort*. Chicago, IL: Unversity of Chicago Press.

Wordes, M., Bynum, T.S., & Conley, C.J. (1994). Locking up youth: The impact of race on detention decisions. *Journal of Research in Crime and Delinquency* 31(2), 149-165.

Woods, L.J. (1988). Home-based family therapy. *Social Work*, 33(3), 211-214.

Wu, B., Cernovich, S., & Dunn, C.S. (1997). Assessing the effects of race and class on juvenile justice processing in Ohio. *Journal of Criminal Justice* 25, 265-277.

ya Azibo, D.A. (1992). Understanding the proper usage and improper usage of the comparative research framework. In A.K.H. Burlew, W.C. Banks, H.P. McAdoo, & D.A. ya Azibo (Eds.) *African-American psychology*. (pp. 18-28). Newbury Park: Sage.

Young, T.M., Dore, M.M., & Pappenfort, D.M. (1989). Trends in residential group care: 1966-1981. In Balcerzak, E.A. (Ed.), *Group care of children: Transitions toward the year 2000*. Washington, D.C.: Child Welfare League of America.

Zehr, H. (1990). *Changing lenses: A new focus for crime and justice*. Scottdale, PA: Herald Press.

Index

Adolescent Coping Orientation for Problem Experiences (ACOPE), 67-71, 76, 80, 86, 90-93

Adaptability, 49, 72-77, 93-94

Adolescent-Family Inventory of Life Events and Changes (A-FILE), 63-66, 80, 86-89, 162

African-American Delinquents, 12-15, 47-48, 83-83, 146

Afrocentric Perspective, 11-15

Boot Camps, 32-34

Coping, 12, 42-52, 56, 60, 66-69, 80, 85, 93, 103-105, 110, 114, 121, 128-130, 137-138, 141-142, 144, 160, 167

Correctional Model, 34-35

Correlations, 53, 62, 81-82, 85, 110-115, 116-120, 139, 163

Delinquency, 2, 7-9, 11-14, 3, 48, 52-54, 57, 140, 153

Disproportionate Minority Confinement, 4-5, 8-10, 17, 41, 43, 49, 83, 145, 149, 151-154, 158

Ecological System(s), 4-6, 15, 27, 29-30, 32, 41-43, 46, 49, 57, 61, 66,
     83-86, 111-114, 123, 127-129, 133-134, 144-147, 154, 160

European-American Delinquents, 2, 7-9, 11-14, 33, 48, 52-54, 57, 140,
     153

Family Adaptability and Cohesion Evaluation Scales II (FACES II),
     62, 70, 72-78, 80, 86, 93-96, 162

Family Adaptability and Cohesion Evaluation Scales III (FACES III),
     72

Family Attachment and Changeability Index 8 (FACI 8), 73, 76-77

Family Cohesion, 13-14, 49-55, 72-74, 80, 86, 105, 138, 147

Family Functioning, 4, 6, 27, 29, 40, 42, 49-52, 56, 59, 66, 70, 74-77,
     80, 85, 95-97, 105, 110, 114-116, 121, 123, 125-127, 130-133,
     136, 138, 142-143, 162

Family Therapy, 26-31, 47, 49-50, 72, 159

Henggler, S., 31

Incremental Validity, 161

Juvenile Court, 26

Kapp, S.A., 3, 9-10, 42, 44, 47, 123, 137, 142, 160

McCubbin, H.I., 42, 44, 47, 63, 65, 67-69, 72-74, 86, 89, 123, 137,
     142, 160, 167

Minuchin, S., 50, 123, 142

Multisystemic Treatment (MST), 31-32

Multiple Regression, 42, 60, 82, 85, 122-134, 162, 164, 167

Olson, D.H., 49, 50, 73-74

Out-of-home placement, 1-6, 26, 28-30, 32, 36, 48-49, 57-58, 60, 78-79, 82-85, 96, 100, 102, 106, 110, 114-115, 121-123, 128. 138-148, 153, 159, 162-163, 166

Parental Control, 14, 49-55, 74-75, 81, 140, 145

Rational Choice Theory, 39

Social Control Theory, 39-40, 140

Stress, 4, 42-52, 56, 59, 63, 65-66, 68, 80, 86-89, 102-103, 108, 110, 121, 125, 130, 136-138, 157, 160

Strain Theory, 37-39, 140, 148, 150-151

Structural Family Therapy, 29-30, 50, 160

Sub-Cultural Deviance Theory, 38, 141

System Dynamics, 4, 147-148, 169, 175-176

Transaction, 41-42, 160

Youth Coping Index (YCI), 69-71